Coaching

D0947771

"This book is a must for any~~...~~ ~~...~~ organizational coaching. It gives a framework for team coaching that will significantly move our industry forward. Importantly it tackles the many complexities that exist in the application of coaching in organizations – whether you sit inside, or outside that organization. It tackles the myths, the metaphors and the realities. As someone whose career has moved from one application of coaching (in sport), to another (now, in business), it has added further understanding to a lifelong journey!"

Adrian Moorhouse, Managing Director, Lane4 & Olympic Gold Medallist

"David's new book is practical and pragmatic and brings in a wealth of research and experience while remaining very readable. It plugs a big gap on my shelf for it is difficult to find a really good book about teams, which David achieves, and he has done this at the same time as showing how coaching can be a powerful approach to team performance and development."

Myles Downey, author of Effective Coaching *and Director of Studies at The School of Coaching*

"I thoroughly recommend *Coaching the Team at Work* to all those interested in individual and organizational development, improving working relationships and above all improving their own capabilities as a learning practitioner. The style is clear and direct, packed with useful and practical advice on how to develop coaching processes to ensure increased effectiveness, whether as a coach, a manager, or a member of the board.

Coaching the Team at Work ranges across a comprehensive range of coaching issues, from the individual to the team, from the strategic to the operational. David Clutterbuck helps to clarify this critical area of organizational learning by providing a plethora of examples and mini case studies, backed up by rigorous research."

Jan Kingsley, Director of Corporate Services, European Foundation for Management Development (EFMD)

Coaching the Team
at Work

DAVID CLUTTERBUCK

NICHOLAS BREALEY
INTERNATIONAL

LONDON · BOSTON

First published by
Nicholas Brealey International in 2007

3–5 Spafield Street
Clerkenwell, London
EC1R 4QB, UK
Tel: +44 (0)20 7239 0360
Fax: +44 (0)20 7239 0370

20 Park Plaza
Boston
MA 02116, USA
Tel: (888) BREALEY
Fax: (617) 523 3708

www.nicholasbrealey.com
www.clutterbuckassociates.com

ISBN-13: 978-1-904838-08-1
ISBN-10: 1-904838-08-1

Library of Congress Cataloging-in-Publication Data
Clutterbuck, David.
    Coaching the team at work / David Clutterbuck.
        p. cm.
    Includes bibliographical references.
    1. Employees--Coaching of. 2. Teams in the workplace--Management. 3.
Organizational learning--Management. 4. Employee motivation. I. Title.
    HF5549.5.C53C58 2007
    658.3'124--dc22

                                                            2006101499

British Library Cataloguing in Publication Data
A catalogue record for this book is available from the
British Library.

Printed in Finland by WS Bookwell.

Contents

CONTENTS

CONTENTS

Introduction

While a great deal has been written about coaching individuals, there has been relatively little investigation of coaching teams at work. Yet in discussions with senior human resource and organizational development professionals, this ability is consistently cited as one of the most serious weaknesses in the capability set of managers at all levels. Even in organizations that have made considerable steps towards becoming coaching cultures,[1] the focus of attention for that coaching is the individual.

However, few people in organizations work alone. Indeed, the whole point of having an organization is to harness the collective efficiency of people working together. Peter Senge makes the point succinctly when he says:

> Knowledge generation . . . primarily occurs in working teams. Individual learning is a by-product of what goes on in really innovative teams. But individual learning is not the goal. In fact, if it becomes the goal, you are in trouble.[2]

Organizations employ teams because they have found that this is a more effective way to organize complex work than any alternative yet designed. Teams provide the bridges between individuals and the organization; and between the need to make localized decisions and customize, and the requirement to adhere to large-scale plans and strategies. Teams also provide the focus of activity that meets people's needs for socialization. They establish the environment where people can share effort, reward and risk. They provide a sense of common identity, rooted in shared ideas, purpose, stories and attitudes. And they provide an opportunity for conversation,

1

support, recognition and other activities that make people feel motivated and raise self-esteem.

Unfortunately, teams don't always live up to their promise. The depressing evidence is that many, if not most, teams in the modern workplace do not harness their collective capability to anything like the extent that they could. Failures of structure and process, lack of purpose or commitment, internal conflict and poor leadership sap the team's potential to work at its optimal level. Some of this loss of performance is inevitable – a simple dynamic of team size, for example – but most is readily manageable, if team members and leaders are minded to reflect intelligently on how they operate and have the skills to do so.

This is where team coaching can be beneficial. It helps teams review performance, boost results, improve communication and build rapport.

Very few goals at team or organizational level can be achieved without some form of performance management process. While addressing the issues that emerge from performance review at an individual level is helpful, in practice most issues involve interaction between team members or in some way have an impact on other members. Addressing performance solely at the level of individuals may be much less effective than engaging all the players in the issue. The more that other team members understand what is needed to help a fellow team member improve performance, the more achievable and sustainable that improvement is likely to be.

Secondly, team coaching, as we shall explore in the following chapters, is a significant part of the remedy for team performance shortfalls. It harnesses a combination of intelligence and curiosity to help teams think through what they are doing and why, how they will integrate individual skill sets and how they will innovate. It also helps the team ask questions that will stimulate the intellectual dialogue necessary for addressing performance issues effectively.

Team coaching also fosters a higher quality of communication, both within the team and between the team and external stakeholders in its activities, ensuring that the dialogue is both intellectual and emotional in character and content. And team coaching promotes the social dialogue that builds rapport, stimulates understanding of self and other team members, and develops the skills to avoid negative conflict and enhance positive conflict within the team.

The aim of this book is to bridge the gap between the limited but growing academic literature on both team learning and team coaching, and the practical experience of managers and workplace coaches. Some of the questions it attempts to answer are:

◆ How is coaching the team different from coaching individuals, and from other processes such as facilitation?
◆ What skills underpin effective team coaching?
◆ What is the responsibility of team members in this process?
◆ How do you know when team coaching has been effective?
◆ When is team coaching appropriate and when will other approaches deliver better results?
◆ How can organizations make team coaching a sustainable, automatic process?

Along the way, we demolish a number of myths about teams and coaching. Among these are the following:

◆ **Teamwork is always better than working alone**. Not true. A whole range of social factors conspires to undermine the efficiencies expected from working collaboratively. Research into team effectiveness suggests that limited collaboration (where everyone does their own thing, with clear guidelines and occasional liaison) often delivers better results than trying to get everybody to work together. Like any other organism, teams are subject to chronic diseases, such as social loafing (where everyone eases off a bit on the assumption that others will take up the slack). Nonetheless, well-managed teams, used in the right circumstances and for the right purposes, are the bedrock of a high-performing organization.

◆ **Coaching is the responsibility of the team leader**. Not true. If coaching is to work, it has to be the responsibility of the team as a whole. There are no spectators. The management of the coaching process belongs to both coaches and coachees.

◆ **The coach is the team leader**. Not necessarily. The role of the team leader is to create the environment where coaching happens, and to provide an example of good coaching practice (as both coach and coachee) for other team members to follow. Peer coaching is as important and frequently more important for a team's success than coaching from the team leader or from someone outside.

◆ **Coaching within the team is an occasional activity**. Not when it's at its most effective. In reality, the more coaching becomes integrated with day-to-day activities and processes, the greater and more lasting its impact on performance.

◆ **Team coaching is about task performance**. Partially true. But *sustainable* improvements in task performance are the result of effective management of three aspects of team focus: achieving the task; managing continuous, relevant learning at both the operational and the wider contextual levels; and managing behaviour within the team and between the team and external stakeholders. It is the integration of these aspects that provides the foundation for teams that are successful over the long term.

About the book

The learning journey of this book follows a logical series of steps – just like coaching – starting with the nature of coaching and ending with helping the team make the decision to self-coach. On the way, we take a variety of detours that seem interesting and relevant – just like coaching. And we try to create insights by asking difficult questions – just like coaching. And if we spend some time in didactic mode, well, it is a book, isn't it? So what do we cover?

In Chapter 1, we review the nature and processes of coaching:

◈ Where does the instinct to coach come from?
◈ How is coaching different from facilitation, mentoring, counselling and other forms of helping people look inwards to learn and grow?
◈ Why has coaching expanded in popularity so dramatically in recent years?
◈ What's the difference between effective and ineffective coaching?

In Chapter 2, we take a look at the nature of the team itself:

◈ What's the difference between a team and a group? Does it matter?
◈ What are the dynamics that underlie team effectiveness and how do they manifest themselves?

Chapter 3 focuses on the role and practice of coaching within the team, answering questions such as:

◈ Who does it? To whom?
◈ When is the best time to coach the team?
◈ How does coaching the team differ from coaching individuals and how can both processes be integrated for the team's collective benefit?
◈ How can the team coach foster a coaching culture?
◈ When is it appropriate for the coach to be the team leader and when should the coach be an external professional?

In Chapter 4, we progress to considering the processes of learning within teams generally and within each of six key team types. We ask:

- What helps and hinders learning?
- How do teams increase the quantity and quality of the learning they experience?
- What should the coach do with each type of team?

In Chapter 5, we examine in more detail the issues that the team coach needs to manage and the skill sets required to do so. We present a framework for organizing team coaching and for developing the relevant skills. Among questions we ask are:

- How do you know you are coaching the team well?
- How do you avoid becoming too cosy?
- What is the right level and kind of conflict for an effective team?

We also offer some suggestions of useful techniques and approaches to cope with common issues that arise in team coaching, relating to the management of interpersonal relationships, temporal issues, and key processes such as goal setting, systems thinking and communication.

Chapter 6 brings the emphasis of team coaching back to the team members, where it belongs, asking:

- How can the team members ensure that they take responsibility for coaching themselves and each other?
- What can they do to assist the leader or an external coach in building the coaching habit?
- What help do both need from the organization?

Throughout the book are case studies drawn from countries as widely separated as Scandinavia, Chile and Australia. They illustrate the variety of approaches used around the world and the potential to learn from others' experiences in an emerging area of knowledge.

This book isn't meant to be a manual for the team coach, whether new in the role or experienced – although it could be used as such. Rather, it is intended to assist those engaged in or aspiring to team coaching in a dialogue that will help them define what team coaching means in their circumstances and environment, the outcomes they expect of it, and how they are going to make it work now and work better in the future.

The essence of coaching is to use the wisdom of the coach to bring to consciousness the wisdom that those being coached hold within themselves. The more we understand how coaching and learning work in a collective context, the more effective our teams will be.

David Clutterbuck
December 2006

CHAPTER ONE

What is coaching?

"A successful coaching engagement will have a cascading effect, creating positive change beyond the person receiving the coaching." | **Diana and Merrill Anderson**[1]

There are various theories about the origins of the word *coach* in the context of people development, but somewhere along the line it shares a common ancestry with *coax*. Coaches act as external stimulators to the potential that other people hold within them. They use a combination of patience, insight, perseverance and caring (sometimes called charisma) to help the coachee(s) find the internal and external resources to improve performance.

Beyond this generic definition, however, lies a wide spectrum of different interpretations about the proper role, behaviours and characteristics of a coach. Depending on circumstances, coaches may need to adopt very different styles to meet the needs of their coachees. Factors that may affect the coaching approach include the complexity of the task, the risks associated with getting the task wrong, the coachee's starting levels of willingness, self-confidence and capability in relation to the task, and the coachee's level of learning maturity (how well they are able to co-manage the coaching process).

All of these factors apply equally to individuals and teams, although in this chapter for simplicity our primary focus is on coaching the individual. Team coaching requires an additional repertoire of approaches and skills, which we will explore in Chapter 3.

Approaches to coaching

Much of the practitioner literature written in recent years attempts to impose one or other perception of coaching as *real*, and to give different labels to other interpretations of the role. This is at best confusing to both coaches and coachees and is disingenuous. The truth is that coaching is multifaceted, multidimensional and highly variable according to purpose and circumstance.

SOME DEFINITIONS OF COACHING

- "Coaching aims to enhance the performance and learning ability of others. It involves providing feedback, but it also uses other techniques such as motivation, effective questioning and matching your management style to the coachee's readiness to undertake a particular task. It is based on helping the coachee to help her/himself through dynamic interaction – it does not rely on a one-way flow of telling and instructing." | **Max Landsberg,** *The Tao of Coaching*[2]

- "Unlocking a person's potential to maximize their own performance... helping them to learn rather than to teach them." | **Sir John Whitmore paraphrasing Timothy Gallwey**

- "Coaching is an ongoing relationship, which focuses on clients taking action towards the realization of their visions, goals or desires." | **US National Optical Astronomy Observatory**

- "Developing a person's skills and knowledge so that their job performance improves, hopefully leading to the achievement of organizational objectives. It targets high performance and improvement at work, although it may also have an impact on an individual's private life. It usually lasts for a short period and focuses on specific skills and goals." | **Chartered Institute of Personnel and Development, UK**

◆ "Working with individuals and small groups to improve their social skills and effectiveness in the workplace." | **Marian Thier**[3]

A useful website for collecting definitions of coaching is the US e-publication Coaching Insider (www.coachinginsider.com). Among the many it offers are:

◆ "A form of training where the supervisor/manager models or demonstrates a behavior or task and uses feedback to guide the employee while she or he practices the behavior or task."

◆ "The process of providing instruction, direction, feedback and support – in order to improve performance and results."

◆ "Coaches provide support, encouragement and help in daily living skills."

◆ "Providing guidance, feedback and direction to ensure successful performance."

◆ "A strategy used to help a client reach her fullest potential and achieve her goals. The coach first helps to define the goals and then supports the client in executing them by mapping out a strategy and helping her stay on track. Coaching helps to balance work, family and social demands as well as leisure and spiritual activities."

◆ "A person who teaches and directs another person via encouragement and advice."

◆ "A relationship between client and coach, in which they collaborate to meet the client's needs. The agenda comes from the client, who is guided and supported in making desirable changes in one or more parts of his or her life, leading to a life that is more fulfilling and more balanced."

◆ "Coaching is essentially a conversation – it is a dialogue between you and I within a productive, results-oriented context. A conversation where, by asking relevant questions at critical junctures, I can encourage and support you to look at different angles and strategies."

◆ "Coaching is about performing at your best through the individual and private assistance of someone who will challenge, stimulate and guide you to keep growing."

◆ "Coaching provides a safe place for clients to identify what is and what is not working, try new behaviors, and learn from their new experiences" | **NASA**

◆ "(Coaches) assist people to identify specific goals and then reach those goals faster and with ease. Provide client with the tools, perspective and structure to accomplish more through a process of accountability. Reframe beliefs and create a point of focus for clients to reflect upon."

◆ "Coaching creates a space of unconditional acceptance where learning, growth and transformation occur naturally as participants (a) find clarity, (b) align with their core values, and (c) take effective action toward meaningful goals. Coaching takes a holistic approach to learning and affirms each participant as whole, capable and resourceful. Spiritual growth is a natural and significant part of the process."

◆ "Coaching is a collaborative, solution-focused, results-orientated systematic process in which the coach facilitates the enhancement of performance, well-being, self-directed learning and personal development of individuals, groups and organisations, who do not have clinically significant mental health issues or abnormal levels of distress." | **Coaching Psychology Unit, University of Sydney**

Not surprisingly, these definitions present a variety of perspectives. Some are quite narrow and close to tutoring (the Coaching Insider website includes a number that equate coaching to pre-examination cramming for students, for example). Some are holistic, seeing coaching as an intervention into any and all areas of an individual's life. Some emphasize what coaching is *not* (e.g. the last of the list represents the real concern that many psychologists have about coaching that oversteps the boundaries appropriate to a non-clinician).[4] Some mention feedback by the coach; others do not mention feedback at all. The common threads, however, are that coaching is a relatively formal relationship that concerns:

- Developing personal (or group) insight
- Performance against specific goals
- Support and encouragement
- Experimentation
- The effective use of questioning skills

Inherent, too, in all the definitions is the concept of a journey – a coach can be seen as a vehicle for taking the individual in the direction they wish to travel.

Part of the reason that there is such variation in interpretation of what a coach is and does is that two models of coaching dominate both literature and practice. The first, most common and most deeply embedded in managerial behaviour, we can call **traditional coaching**. The salient elements of this kind of coaching can be summarized as follows:

- The coach helps the learner clarify the goal they wish to achieve. Frequently, this goal, or the relevant level of performance required, is not one that the learner has defined. In a line-manager-as-coach role, the goal may be a performance requirement resulting from team targets or a general competence framework. In sports, the standard required at various levels from beginner to master is typically set by a governing body. This same body may also set standards for the competence of coaches.

- The coach agrees with the learner what they will do to achieve the desired level of performance. This typically requires a plan of activity that includes practice.
- The coach either observes the activity or monitors the outcome and uses this information to help the learner identify faults or modify their approach. This may involve direct feedback or a review discussion, in which the learner creates their own feedback through guided reflection on what happened.
- The cycle repeats itself. Gradually, in effective coaching, the learner develops the confidence to experiment on their own initiative and to bring more and more of their own observation and reflection to the review process, until the coach's intervention is no longer required.

Those who describe themselves as "executive coaches" are often sniffy about traditional coaching, in spite of its long pedigree in the workplace. They espouse a model that we can call **developmental coaching**, which has its origins in Socratic dialogue[5] but is more recently derived from a mixture of European developmental mentoring practices and behavioural science. The core of this model is that the coach:

- Uses skilled questioning to help the learner develop an understanding of the situation, the processes at work within it and the internal and external forces working to encourage or discourage performance.
- Helps the learner build and sustain the motivation to pursue chosen goals.
- Is available for further stimulation and reflexive questioning as and when the learner needs it.

Sandwiched between these two models of coaching are many hybrids. Some executive coaches base their practice on a combination of observation of executives at work followed by feedback, but with a Socratic style to the reviewing process. Many coaches in both sport and technical training like to demonstrate, so the coachee initially observes, and to maintain an iteration of observe—try for yourself—discuss how it went—observe again. Others adopt what we can call a "suggest" style, focusing the coachee on what to observe about both their own performance, behaviours and feelings and those of other people. Indeed, it is sometimes helpful to think of styles of coaching as a spectrum from directiveness to non-directiveness, ranging from **tell** (instruct, observe and give feedback), through **sell** (demonstrate, observe and give feedback) and **suggest** (focusing the learner's experimentation and observation, but using self-feedback), to stimulate or **ask** (encouraging the learner through effective questioning to manage their own experimentation and observation). These alternative styles map fairly neatly onto the learner's starting point, as shown in Figure 1.1.

FIGURE 1.1

FOUR APPROACHES TO COACHING

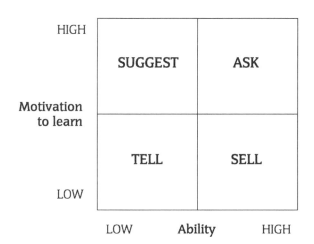

Yet others recognize all these approaches as valid and have developed competences in all of them. These flexible coaches have the capacity to adapt to a wide range of circumstances and coachees'

requirements. They typically assess where the coachee is starting from in terms of motivation and ability and gradually shift style as the circumstances change.

BECOMING AN INSPIRING PRESENTER

For example, a newly appointed director had recently been panned in audience feedback for his presentation at his company's annual "top 100" meeting. His presentation was described as uninspiring, rambling and difficult to hear. Communication skills were tacked on to the list of issues his executive coach would work through with him.

The coach used a stimulating (ask) style to identify the specific communication problems and establish a set of improvement goals, which the director would work through with the company's public relations manager, who would act as a subject expert. After six months, the content and appearance of the PowerPoint™ slides had improved (the PR department took over the production), but little further progress had been made. The coach and the director agreed to put the issue aside for the moment, as there were more urgent needs relating to sorting out the director's team and because he was not highly motivated to address the problem.

Two months before the next top 100 meeting, the CEO made it clear that he wanted to bring the issue much higher up the director's agenda. The PR manager suggested bringing in a second coach, one who specialized in communication skills. The first thing this coach did was drill into the reasons for the director's low motivation to address the problem, by exploring the emotions he felt whenever he had to give a speech. The dominant emotion was fear. The communication coach agreed with the director to ignore the presentation skills concerns until the emotional base had changed. The style of coaching agreed on to start with was tell, because the director's fear was so great that he could not self-observe, or even try to copy other people.

The company was about to begin a round of presentations to the investment community, so these became a platform for real but relatively unthreatening practice. The director took a small part in each of these meetings, with the size of his role expanding as the series progressed and as the size of the audience grew from two or three people to 25 or so. The communication coach and fellow directors gave direct feedback immediately following each session.

After a few weeks, the director had gained sufficient confidence to be open to a mixture of observing others and observing himself. A couple of presentations were videoed and the coach discussed these with him in detail. Gradually, the director began to see the slideshow and the lectern not as essential props (in the sense of propping him up) but as hindrances to free interchange with the audience. His growing confidence – both in himself and in his knowledge of what he was talking about – allowed him to deliver a much more relaxed, better-received presentation this time.

This wasn't the end of the learning journey, however. Now that he and the coach had progressed to a stimulator (ask) style, they were able to address a range of issues relating to his role as a communicator and as a champion of effective communication within his division. How was he going to ensure that there were effective communication strategies? How could he bring about improvements in the quality of day-to-day communication within his division, especially with regard to employees who worked in small, remote teams?

By the time the communication coach had moved on, the director had established a new and much more productive relationship with the PR manager and his CEO. The next year, he co-led the team making presentations to investors.

Coaching compared to mentoring

Another source of confusion is between coaching and mentoring. In practice, the skills of developmental coach and developmental mentor have many similarities. They both help people work towards goals by building their self-awareness, strengthening their motivation and providing emotional support. What distinguishes the approaches primarily is the difference in the purpose of the relationship. Put simply, coaching answers the question: "What do you want to improve in?" Mentoring answers the question: "What (or who) do you want to become?" Somewhere in between – depending on the nature of the goal – lies the question: "What do you want to achieve?"

At an executive level in particular, developmental coaching is also distinguished from developmental mentoring in the following ways:

◆ Coaching is typically of much shorter duration, working on a specific improvement goal, such as presentation skills, managing meetings or developing particular attributes of leadership. It may be triggered either by a problem or an opportunity. Mentoring, on the other hand, typically has a much more open agenda and longer-term goals. Often goals identified in mentoring lead to coaching interventions. Mentoring almost always focuses on long-term opportunities, although it may also deal with current problems, in the context of achieving the longer-term change.

◆ Developmental coaches tend to avoid giving advice. Developmental mentors also typically hold back on giving advice, helping the mentee to think matters through for themselves first, but they are willing and able to advise, based on their experience, when appropriate.

◆ Developmental mentoring includes a wider spectrum of roles than coaching, including being a sounding board, helping the mentee develop wider and better networks of information and influence (i.e. helping them become more self-resourceful) and sometimes simply being there to listen and empathize.

Coaching and mentoring in all their manifestations are both about achieving change. They harness change processes that people can manage for themselves and make these more powerful by:

◆ Enhancing the person's awareness of what is happening, both within them and around them
◆ Helping them through the process of commitment (sometimes by being the person they commit to)
◆ Expressing belief in their ability to make the change
◆ Supporting them through the inevitable points of relapse
◆ Working on the quality of their thinking

Coaching compared to counselling and therapy

Coaching is also sometimes confused with counselling or therapy. It's true that coaches may use similar techniques to counsellors or therapists, but in general they need to be aware of the boundaries that it is dangerous to cross. Coaches who blunder into areas of therapeutic need where they lack specialist expertise have been lambasted in various articles as irresponsible and dangerous.[6]

Australian psychologist Anthony Grant[7] defines several key differences between coaching and therapy:

◆ Coaching deals with clients who are basically functional, although dissatisfied with some aspect of their lives, or who aspire to reach higher levels of performance; therapy deals with people who are in some manner dysfunctional or have psychological problems.
◆ Coaching emphasizes finding solutions, rather than unravelling and understanding problems and difficulties. Coaching is therefore more future focused, while therapy tends to be more past focused.
◆ Coaching doesn't deal with clinical issues, such as depression.

Interestingly, many therapists and counsellors now argue that coaching is an important part of their toolkit, or should be. Equally, effective coaches need enough understanding of human psychology and behaviour to recognize danger signs and refer clients on where appropriate.

Taking an integrated approach

One of the problems with taking a narrow view of coaching is that the opportunity may be lost to enrich practice with ideas, approaches and philosophies from other, related disciplines. Psychologist and coach Pauline Willis, of the Coaching and Mentoring Network, uses the model in Figure 1.2 to illustrate how the various disciplines interrelate with coaching and mentoring.

A set of core personal and professional competences sit in the middle of the diagram and around the outside there is a band of competences drawn from the specialist professional domains described. A coaching psychologist would be qualified in one or more specialist areas of psychology, for example. The domains described and the specific competences given are illustrative – a lot more could be added – but Willis's approach allows for a much wider debate than normally occurs about the scope and nature of coaching and about the knowledge and skills base on which coaches can draw.

Both coaches and those who employ them will benefit from ensuring that they have a clear understanding of when it is appropriate for coaching to be context independent and when the context demands a form of specialist intervention. In many cases, it happens that a client requires more than one type of help – perhaps a business coach to help think through issues relating to strategy and a broad personal development agenda, and a psychological coach to address particular behavioural patterns that prevent them achieving their full potential.

FIGURE 1.2

THE INTEGRATED MODEL OF COACHING AND MENTORING COMPETENCE

Presented to the Coaching Psychology Forum in 2003.

For example, a CEO being coached around building a new team also needed help to deal with his inability to confront and manage aggressive women. The roots of this problem lay in his maternal relationship as a child and were outwith the role and competence of the business coach, who referred him on to a behavioural psychologist with experience in similar issues.

The key steps in a coaching intervention

A coaching intervention can be seen as comprising seven steps, as in Table 1.1.

TABLE 1.1

THE SEVEN STEPS OF THE COACHING INTERVENTION

1   Identify the need to improve/change
2   Observe and gather evidence
3   Motivate to set and own personal improvement targets
4   Help to plan how to achieve those targets
5   Create opportunities to practise the desired skills
6   Observe in action and give objective feedback
7   Help to work through setbacks

Identify the need to improve/change

All coaching starts with a need for change. Usually it is the coachee who determines and owns that need, but sometimes it is imposed by another party – a line manager, a close friend or relative, or society in general. The need may be very specific (e.g. meet defined targets for sales or customer satisfaction) or much broader (e.g. become a more effective team leader). It may be short term or long term.

Typically at this stage the need will not be sufficiently well defined to be classified as a clear performance goal; or the *what* may be clear, but the *how* much less so. I sometimes describe the phenomenon as "performance itch": knowing you could and perhaps should perform better, but not as yet having addressed and thought about the issue in depth.

Observe and gather evidence

Before tackling the performance issue, it is important that the coachee understands both what performance they should be (or want to be) aiming at, and the critical sub-areas of performance that hold them back. For example, in the sport of fencing a failure to hit the opponent is often caused by poor arm movement, which is itself a result of poor foot placement. Understanding the sequence of performance-influencing events requires observation, often over several sequences of the same task or situation. This initial feedback and analysis can come from a number of sources: an expert coach, working colleagues (particularly through 360-degree feedback) and from the individual themselves.

Some of the most dramatic changes in managerial behaviour have come about by using a technique I call scripting, in which the coachee writes down the text of encounters that go wrong and that seem to follow the same pattern of verbal exchanges. They also note down their feelings at each point in the conversation. Almost invariably, common repeated patterns emerge when they compare scripts from different occasions. With the help of a coach, they can determine which elements of the script they want to change and in what order.

Direct observation from a trained coach has the advantage of objectivity. In addition, the coach is usually able to draw on experience to identify real or potential causal factors that may not be apparent to the coachee or their peers. In general, the more sources of initial feedback the coachee is able to harness, the more useful and credible the evidence on which they can build.

Motivate to set and own personal improvement targets

The step between recognizing an opportunity for personal change and doing something about it can be large. Most of us have a multitude of areas of knowledge, behaviour or skill where we can see potential benefits from improving our performance. Whether we will seriously engage in making those changes happen and in sustaining them relates to:

- The value we attach to achieving the change and the expected benefits that will flow from it.
- The degree of confidence we feel in our ability and the likelihood of achieving the change.
- The amount of effort we expect to have to put into the change.

The equation underlying the extent of motivation for change is essentially as follows:

| Perceived benefits of change (PBC) | - | Perceived effort/cost (PEC) | + | Likelihood of achievement (LA) | = | Motivation to change |

See also Figure 1.3, which considers the degree of motivation on a 1–5 scale: the larger the grey zone, the stronger the learner's motivation.

FIGURE 1.3

THE ZONE OF MOTIVATION

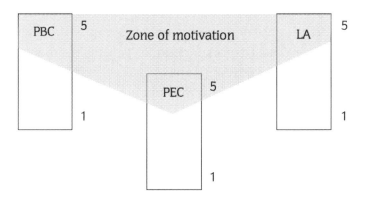

Moderating the perceived effort/cost and the perceived benefits may also be the perceived *risk* (a good coaching question is: "What's the risk of succeeding?"). Other relevant coaching questions include:

◆ How important is this to the coachee's self-image? The more the perceived change aligns with their sense of an ideal self, the more important it may be to the individual to make the change.

◆ What will they have to stop doing in order to make the change happen? In a full life or a hectic working environment, there is often simply no room to add new goals or activities without dropping some existing ones.

Help to plan how to achieve those targets

It is at this point that the coaching conversation comes into its own (more on this below). The critical steps include:

◆ **Clarifying outcomes** (what does the coachee want to happen and what do they want to avoid happening?). This is about more than establishing goals (the G of GROW; see below). It also relates to re-examining and developing self-awareness around one's motivations and how these link to both overt and unspoken values. The coach helps the coachee envision what success will look like. Important questions include:
  ❏ What will achieving this do in terms of helping you to your next objective?
  ❏ Will success open out more options for you or close options down?
  ❏ Who else has a stake in this?

◆ **Mapping the influencing context**: the internal and external drivers and barriers to achieving and sustaining the desired change. These factors may be internal (for example the coachee's level of self-confidence); or they may relate to infield players (working colleagues whose help will be needed) or to outfield players (people who exert a more distant influence and/or stake in the change). The coach helps the coachee develop a greater level of understanding of each of these influencers, how they work, and the degree to which the coachee can overcome barriers and harness drivers.

◆ **Chunking up and down**. Chunking in the coaching sense relates to either breaking down the learning task into manageable elements, or bringing apparently discrete issues together to create a larger, more aspirational task. The coach helps the coachee recognize the task constituents and prioritize the order in which to tackle them.

◆ **Establishing how you and the coachee will know you are making progress**. Coaching questions include:

- ❏ What milestones can you set along the way?
- ❏ How will you and others assess that you have achieved these?
- ❏ How will you feel?
- ❏ What will other people tell you?
- ❏ What will you be doing differently?
- ❏ What will other people be doing differently?

Create opportunities to practise the desired skills

Whether the opportunity to practise is created by a line manager or by the coachee themselves, once the plan emerges it is important to implement it rapidly. The longer it takes, the easier it is for commitment to seep away.

Observe in action and give objective feedback

The primary difference between feedback at this point and feedback earlier in the process is that the former is more specific and more focused. The closer the feedback is to the point of practice, the more impact it is likely to have. A secondary difference is that in giving feedback at this point, the effective coach gradually shifts the emphasis from extrinsic feedback (feedback to the coachee) to intrinsic feedback (by the coachee to themselves). The more the reflective dialogue is based on intrinsic feedback, the readier the learner is to move on to new challenges.

Help to work through setbacks

The story of personal change is peppered with setbacks. Sometimes you can predict these by effective analysis of the context, and prepare tactics to manage each situation as it arises. But at other times the coachee will feel discouraged, perhaps ready to give up. The effective coach recognizes that setbacks will occur, prepares the learner for the event, and gives support and empathy through the seven-step process of Review, Reaffirmation, Regroup, Revalue, Retarget, Resource and Relaunch:

- Under **review**, the coach ensures that the coachee has opportunities to discuss progress and is getting the extrinsic feedback they need, and encourages them to take time to reflect on their progress.
- **Reaffirmation** involves building the coachee's confidence in their ability to achieve the desired change and overcome the obstacles.
- The coach helps the coachee **regroup** by assisting them to step back from the issue, take stock of what has been achieved (often more than the learner has admitted to themselves) and take a reality check.
- In **revaluing**, the coachee re-examines their motivations and drives to improve – are these still as strong? If not, what could remotivate the coachee?
- **Retargeting** is about recalibrating and refocusing. If the goal cannot be reached in three months, can it be done in six? If the

coachee can't get the promotion they want now, what alternative role would give them job satisfaction and position them to achieve a similar role, perhaps in another company?

◆ Evaluating the **resources** available to the coachee helps them consider how and where they will find additional support for the changes they want to make.

◆ Finally, **relaunching** looks at how the coachee will get back on the road with renewed enthusiasm and energy.

FIGURE 1.4

SEVEN STEPS IN COPING WITH SETBACKS

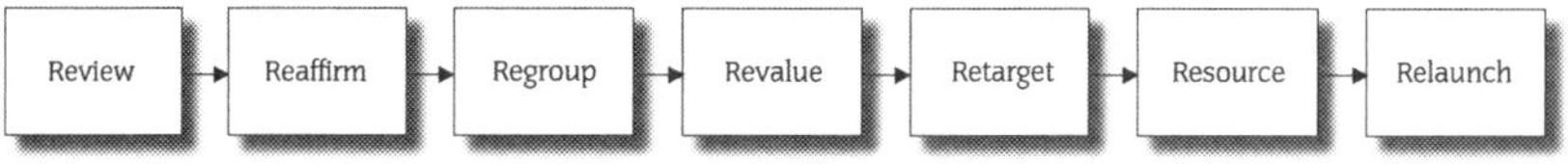

Review	Reaffirm	Regroup	Revalue	Retarget	Resource	Relaunch

The coaching conversation

There are several models that describe the coaching conversation. The most commonly used is Sir John Whitmore's GROW[8] – standing for Goals, Reality, Options, Will – which simplifies a raft of former observations about learning dialogue. Although many people tend to follow the four steps in the order of the acronym, in practice effective coaches intermingle them, based on observation of where it will be most helpful for the client to start.

My own studies of coaching and mentoring focus on the coaching conversation as a learning dialogue, a theme that has been explored by Argyris,[9] Schon, and many other observers of managerial behaviour. The experience of coaches and mentors suggests that there are seven levels of dialogue[10] that they may use in helping the learner build understanding, identify ways forward and take control of their own development:

◆ The first level of learning dialogue is **social**, aimed at building rapport and hence the trust that underpins effective learning relationships.

◆ **Technical** dialogue helps the coachee understand the systems and processes essential to doing the task.

◆ **Tactical** dialogue helps them work out practical ways to deal with issues they meet at work or in other aspects of their lives – for example how to cope with excessive demands on their time from two bosses.

◆ **Strategic** dialogue takes the process deeper, providing an opportunity to examine the context and big picture behind an issue and developing longer-term solutions.

◆ Dialogue for **self-insight** changes the focus of conversation from the external environment to the internal. For example, it examines how the coachee is contributing to the problems they experience, helps work out what they really want from a set of difficult circumstances and encourages self-belief.

◆ Dialogue for **behavioural change** builds on these insights to apply both externally and internally focused insights and achieve a structured plan for adapting the coachee to their environment.

◆ **Integrative** dialogue ranges across all the other levels in a search for greater personal meaning and a deeper understanding of the coachee's role and purpose, in both work and non-work contexts.

All of these levels relate to some extent to improving performance and developing greater competence. Integrative dialogue is perhaps most closely associated with mastery, or to be more precise an appreciation of mastery. Each level is also dependent to a greater or lesser extent on those below it. If there is no rapport from social dialogue, the quality of tactical dialogue suffers – for example, we accept advice more easily from a salesperson we trust than from one who may be more knowledgeable; it's hard to be truly strategic without some understanding of tactics; and planned behaviour change without self-knowledge is an uphill struggle. The higher the level of dialogue, the deeper will be the impact on the individual.

Outside the chain of dialogue is the normal transactional conversation that dominates most work-based interactions. Transactional conversations do not seek shared meaning; they occur to facilitate instruction (in both senses of the word) and monitoring. Such exchanges are important and useful, but they have little or no positive impact on the way people think or the attitudes they display. (There is also a "hygiene" effect in the sense that peremptory instructions can breed resentment and passive resistance.)

The effective coach needs to understand the level of dialogue appropriate to the specific role and their own capability to work at each level. Not surprisingly, the proportion of coaches able to work competently at the integrative level is relatively small. It has been suggested that the skills increase required in moving from one level to the next is a logarithmic scale, with each step being three times as difficult as the one before. A problem for the coaching profession is that while, for example, life coaches realistically need to operate at the level of integrative dialogue, many people claiming to fulfil the role are not adequately able to progress beyond the tactical or strategic level.

Underlying all the seven layers of the coaching conversation are a number of basic principles, set out below.

PRINCIPLES OF THE COACHING CONVERSATION

- ◆ Listening for understanding – expecting to have assumptions and customary views challenged and changed as listening goes deeper.

- ◆ Encouraging others to be explicit about the way their reasoning links up, and testing the assumptions that arise on the way.

- ◆ Doing the same openly with one's own thinking.

- Challenging by being open and frank and by encouraging the other person to do the same; respecting what they say when they take up the challenge.

- Being willing to own one's view clearly as well as evoking the other person's; being indifferent as to which view the other adopts. Exploring what is unsaid and the implications of this for the coaching relationship and also in the rest of the coachee's world.

What good coaches do

Coaching competences have been the subject of a number of recent studies, most notably an international project by the European Mentoring and Coaching Council to capture the perspectives of practitioners from a wide range of disciplines and schools of thought. One of the conclusions that can be drawn from this on-going work is that there are indeed some generic coaching competences, along with a vast array of specific competences, most of which derive from a combination of the type of issues and circumstance being tackled and the discipline or background through which people have arrived at coaching. Something about having only a hammer and seeing all problems as needing a nail automatically comes to mind at this point. If you have spent years learning the intricacies of gestalt therapy, it's hard not to see every client through that lens, for example. I have seen at least one professional coach routinely gestalt his clients into submission without thought of whether a different approach might be appropriate! In our work helping organizations select executive coaches to work with their senior managers, one of the key criteria we apply is: "Does this person have a sufficiently wide portfolio of approaches to meet the needs of this organization and its managers?"

A second conclusion that can be drawn is that, just as there are levels of coaching dialogue, so there are levels of coaching function.

TABLE 1.2

COMPETENCES OF COACHES AT DIFFERENT LEVELS OF OPERATION

LEVEL	CONSTITUENT COMPETENCES
Level 1: Delivering day-to-day coaching in the workplace as part of general performance management	• Understanding of coaching theory • Basic listening skills • Basic skills of observing and assessing performance • Basic skills of giving feedback • Ability to set and motivate people to pursue performance goals • Motivating reluctant learners • Encouraging people to coach and support each other in learning • Skills of social, technical, tactical and strategic dialogue • Demonstrating good practice, where appropriate
Level 2: Working with individuals or teams to achieve significant improve-ments in a specific range of skills – physical, technical or behavioural	Over and above Level 1: • Understanding of learning theory and motivational theory • Advanced skills of listening • Advanced skills of giving feedback • Skills of dialogue for self-insight and behaviour change • Specialist knowledge and experi-ence in the performance area (e.g. in a specific sport or area of IT)
Level 3: Assisting an individual in achieving a personal transformation	Over and above Levels 1 and 2: • Broader understanding of behavioural theory • Having a wide portfolio of behavioural models • At least basic skills of integrative dialogue • Counselling skills

These can be described as:

◆ **Level 1**: Delivering day-to-day coaching in the workplace as part of general performance management, typically by a line manager or team colleague.
◆ **Level 2**: Working with individuals or teams to achieve significant improvement in a specific range of skills – physical, technical or behavioural.
◆ **Level 3**: Assisting an individual in achieving a personal transformation.

Some generic skills relevant to each level are suggested in Table 1.2. This is not meant to be an exhaustive list but a practical general template, to be amended in line with circumstances. Within each of the three suggested levels, it is also possible to draw further distinctions: for example various professional bodies have drawn up gradations of competence relating to Level 3, to establish a development ladder for executive coaches.

Competences of the coachee

Coaching is an activity done *with* someone, not *to* someone. So the responsibility for making the learning process work is shared between the coach and the coachee. Both need to demonstrate the behaviours of trust and openness essential for rapport; both need to listen, reflect and seek understanding; and both need to have a sense of ownership of the outcomes. Most coaching programmes or initiatives in organizations ignore the contribution of the coachee in managing and drawing success out of the coaching intervention, yet enhancing the coachee's competence in and motivation for the task is also important.

So what are the critical skills of a coachee? As with the coach, some will be situational, but generic skills include the abilities in Table 1.3.

TABLE 1.3

COMPETENCES OF THE COACHEE

Articulating the issues on which they need help, the progress they are making and how they would like the coach to assist. Our research suggests that explaining what form of help they need has a strong and positive impact on the style, focus and management of the coaching dialogue, because it gives the coach a practical starting point. Effective coaches often ensure that the first stage of the dialogue establishes both what the issue is and where the coachee has reached in their understanding and dealing with it, by asking the coachee what kind of conversation they feel would be most beneficial.

Reflecting on the issue, both before and after the coaching conversation. It's important for the coachee to be able to prepare in terms of thinking through what the real issues are, identifying and describing examples, and determining what outcomes they want..

Listening actively – this also includes asking for time to think at key points in the coaching conversation.

Being open about both the rational and the emotional elements of the issue. It's much harder for the coach to help if the coachee is not willing or able to be honest and unsecretive about what they think and what they feel. Being open also involves being honest with oneself and able to consider alternative ideas and perspectives.

Managing challenge – from the coach, from oneself, to the coach and to other stakeholders. There is a portfolio of sub-skills here relating to personal confidence, self-insight, goal management and so on. For coaching by team leaders or team managers, the coachee needs to have the courage and capability to ask for coaching and to persevere until it is forthcoming.

Relationship management – for example giving and earning respect, establishing and maintaining rapport.

Proactive learning – for example translating the coaching conversation into action, developing a network of learning resources, and reviewing progress against learning goals.

To some extent the development of these skills can be part of the coaching agenda. But the range, depth and value of the coaching dialogue can be much greater when the coachee already has these capabilities. And when individuals come together in a team, lack of any of these skills in some or all of these areas may reduce the effectiveness of team coaching.

Before we can investigate the additional skills required for coaching a team, we need to establish a base of understanding about the nature and workings of teams.

CHAPTER TWO

Defining the team

"Some teams work hard, have fun and get the job done. Other teams are miserable and ineffective, despite the fact that all the team members are working twice as hard as normal. Why is this?" | **Max Landsberg in** *The Tao of Coaching*

Behavioural scientists and others have been fascinated by the nature of teams for over a century and many of the most famous social experiments, such as the Hawthorne project,[1] have been aimed at creating insight into the processes that make teams effective and ineffective. From the perspective of the coach, understanding the fundamental dynamics, both of teams in general and of the teams with which they or their clients work, is an important part of the knowledge and skills set. This chapter is not intended to be an exhaustive review of the vast literature on teams. Rather, it attempts to identify and discuss those themes of which the team coach needs to be particularly aware.

So what do we know about teams that will be helpful to the coach? To answer this question, we need first to define what we mean by a team, which is by no means as straightforward as it seems. Then we need to review the key themes about the structure, dynamics and behaviour of teams that emerge from the hundreds of studies in recent decades, and determine how these might affect the coaching role and task. Finally, we take a brief look at how teams evolve.

Let's start with the definition!

What is a team?

In many ways, it is easier to describe what a team is *not* than what it is. In particular, a team is both different to and more than a group. Members of a group may not consciously see themselves as connected. For example, a mentoring programme aimed at the homosexual community within a large company foundered rapidly when gays and lesbians made it clear that they did not want to be classed together. Members of a group give higher priority to personal goals than group goals and feel freer to take unilateral action, without consideration of collective needs or welfare.

The *Penguin English Dictionary* defines a group as:

> "A number of objects or people, which can be regarded as a collective unit or as sharing certain characteristics; number of people sharing views, social customs, beliefs, etc."

A well-regarded academic definition[2] is that work groups are "intact social systems that perform one or more tasks within an organizational context".

Hence we do not talk of a team of shareholders or a team of hobbyists: sharing a specific common interest and taking collective action to achieve a common goal (e.g. the sacking of an unpopular company chairman) may require a certain amount of collaboration and co-planning, but it does not form the basis for continuing mutual interaction and supportiveness.

A team brings something extra to the nature and quality of the interaction between members of a group. One of the most commonly quoted definitions comes from Jon Katzenbach,[3] a severe critic of the common confusion between teams and groups:

> "A small number of people with complementary skills, who are committed to a common purpose, performance goals

and approach, for which they hold themselves mutually accountable."

Taking the key elements of this definition in turn, it is clear that teams have a limitation in terms of **size**. The more people involved, the more complex the interactions and hence the less able the group (for that's what it is) is to function. Groups can coordinate large numbers of people – for example in a military march-past or a Mexican wave in a rugby stadium – but the interaction has to be relatively simple. Who is in or out of the team can vary according to context. For example, a football team may variously be interpreted as the players currently on the field, those players plus their colleagues waiting on the bench, the full squad, the direct support network of coaches, counsellors, physiotherapists and other specialists, or wider still the full staff and volunteers maintaining the pitch and selling programmes. The narrower the definition, the smaller the unit and the more clearly the other team characteristics can be seen.

Complementary skills are important, because they allow more value to be created by harnessing a range of talent and knowledge.

Commitment to a common purpose emphasizes the requirement for a shared sense of direction. Without a common purpose, individual priorities and intentions will dominate what people do and there will be little coordination.

Commitment to the same performance goals is similarly needed to ensure that everyone has the same understanding of what the outcomes of their work should be.

A TEAM OF COMPUTERS?

A classic example of team failure in commitment to the same goals occurred in a heavy engineering factory in the UK. A mixed "team" of sales and production staff was formed to oversee the progress of customer projects from order to delivery. Unfortunately, both sides retained their previous perceptions about priorities. The sales people insisted that rapid turnaround and meeting customer deadlines – no matter how demanding – were most important; the production people focused instead on cost minimization by ensuring long production runs. The team was eventually abandoned in favour of a computerized mediation system!

Commitment to a common approach concerns *how* the team manages its tasks. Conflict about method or process is very common, because people tend to assume that the way they have always done things, being tried and tested, is the best way.

Mutual accountability is the other side of the coin to mutual commitment. One of the biggest problems with a command-and-control style of management, for example, is that people delegate responsibility upwards.

Katzenbach's definition is just one of many, however. Leigh Thompson,[4] whose extensive review of the operation and psychology of teams has become a standard text, describes a team as:

> "a group of people, who are interdependent with respect to information, resources and skills, and who seek to combine their efforts to achieve a common goal."

Thompson draws for his definition on Hackman,[5] who maintains that:

- Teams exist to achieve a shared goal.
- Members depend on each other to achieve the goal.
- They have boundaries (it's clear who is in the team and who is not).
- They are stable over time.
- They have authority to manage their own work and internal processes.
- They operate in a social systems context (they are part of a larger organization, to whose goals they contribute or which they attempt to influence).

Let's look at some of these characteristics in more detail.

- **Goals**. Who sets the shared goal for a team? In the work context, the goal may be imposed from above and the cohesion of the team may depend on the degree of collective motivation that the goal inspires in them. A goal may motivate some members of the team more than others and this can undermine the team's performance. In addition, individual goals may conflict with team goals and team goals with organizational goals. In forming a team from a group, the members agree to subordinate some or all of their own goals to the collective goal.
- **Interdependence**. Just as team members may vary in their attachment to the team's goals, the extent of their dependence on each other may also vary. Just because people depend on each other to perform specific tasks does not necessarily make them a team. In a mass-production factory, a failure by one worker on the line has consequences for people in subsequent stages. But to become a team, those on the line must actively collaborate and seek to manage the process together, rather than be managed by it. Charlie Chaplin's notable parody *Modern Times* illustrates what happens when this collaborative process management is absent.
- **Boundaries**. The boundaries of the team are not just a matter of who is on the payroll. Top teams, for example, may include a shadow director in the form of an influential consultant (or a coach). Equally, there may be boundaries within the team, cliques who have a separate sub-identity by virtue of the specialist tasks they perform or the greater comradeship they feel towards some colleagues compared to others. What seems to matter is a collective sense of the membership and of what constitutes an insider or an outsider. Without that collective sense of identity, the team is likely to disintegrate rapidly.
- **Stability**. Hackman's views on stability as a critical characteristic of a team are not supported by our research into learning

approaches within different types of team (see Chapter 4). Not every team is stable, either in membership or longevity. Many teams are created for specific, short-term tasks. Membership of a team may change rapidly. In one organization, I asked an audience of 60 managers how many of them had been in the same team for more than six months. Only a few raised their hands. Yet all were certain that they were currently part of a team. Another example of a team that is unstable in both membership and duration is a rugby side like the Barbarians – composed of players from different nations, who would never normally play alongside each other, they can quickly gel into a formidable unit, exhibiting all the other qualities of a team. This coherence of collaboration continues even when members are substituted during the course of the game. It seems that ability to adhere to shared collaborative routines is more relevant as a factor than stability *per se*.

◆ **Being part of a social system**. This brings both blessings and curses. The organization can provide support, resources and wider cultural norms that help define appropriate behaviour. But it can also impose restrictions, limiting access to resources and imposing rules that undermine the team's efforts, or are seen to do so. Systems designed for the convenience of the organization as a whole may not work in favour of the effectiveness of the team, and vice versa. For example, it may be to the benefit of the organization that the most talented team members are promoted to new roles elsewhere. If the team sees this as damaging, it is likely to lead to a reduction in performance; if, on the other hand, it sees it as a welcome opportunity to bring in new blood, with new ideas and skills, then the opposite may be the case.

In our research, we asked a mixture of team leaders, team members and human resource professionals to describe how they saw the difference between working in a team and working in a group. The responses they gave included most of the characteristics above, but also a number of additional ingredients. In particular, members of a team:

◆ Use more structured and more varied forms of communication than members of groups. Team members communicate on a number of levels, both formal and informal, and invest energy in maintaining the quality of communication.

◆ Offer and seek support from each other. Team members recognize when other members need help and/or encouragement, and take time away from their own task priorities to assist their colleagues.

◆ Accept personal discomfort or disadvantage, where there is a clash between their own interests and those of the team as a whole, for example holding back on getting a new computer because another team member's need is more urgent.

◆ Adapt roles and behaviours to the needs of the task and of their colleagues. Some types of work (e.g. assembly-line manufacture) lend themselves less well to such flexibility, but all genuine teams have a capacity for people to adapt what they do to meet the requirements of different situations.

Types of team

Most studies and writing about teams not only confuse groups with teams, they also assume that a team is a team is a team. Analogies are drawn between teams in one context – for example sport or music – and the work context, with little recognition or appreciation of the difference in purpose, structure or fundamental dynamics between them. Even within the work context, there are very big differences between teams, which the coach needs to recognize and to take into account when devising interventions.

The analogy between coaching at work and in sport is both commonplace and often misleading. The sporting analogy sees the coach as a leader on the touchline, someone who helps the team build its confidence and competence, but has to stand back and let it perform well or badly on its own. On the field, it is the captain who takes the lead and their role is separate from that of the coach. This model can be seen in organizations, where an external coach is brought in to work with the team and its leader, or sometimes with the leader alone. But in the workplace, it is far more common to expect the team leader and team coach to be one and the same person.

An acute observer of the sports analogy, Robert Keidel, points out that sports teams are different from each other in structure and dynamics, too. He provides a catalogue of corporate disasters resulting from leaders imposing an inappropriate sports model on their organizations. Baseball, American football and basketball may seem superficially similar, but they differ in several fundamental ways.

First, the level of interdependence is different. In baseball, team member contributions are relatively independent of each other. Only a few of the players are involved in the action at any time. (Cricket is similar.) The success of the team depends to a high degree on the performance of individuals. Keidel calls this **pooled interdependence**. American football involves **sequential interdependence** to achieve a steady drive forward across the lines. Success depends on the cooperation of members of specialist subgroups within the team. Basketball requires **reciprocal interdependence**: each player has to be ready to assist the others in a largely unpredictable flow of play. The basic unit is therefore the team itself.

Secondly, the density of players is very low in baseball, where they are spread out across the field. In American football, the players are bunched together. In basketball, where "players are coupled to their team-mates in a fluid, unfolding manner", they are densest of all.

Keidel maintains that these factors have implications for team management in three ways: coordination, management competence and development focus. Coordination in baseball is achieved mainly through the formal structure and intricate rules of the game; in American football it is achieved through "planning and hierarchical direction"; and in baseball by mutual adjustment by the players.

The role of the manager and/or coach in baseball is to create the environment where each player can perform at their best. It therefore requires a relatively light touch with regard to supervision and control, but a high concentration on developing the individual. By contrast, the role of the manager and/or coach in American football is heavily hands-on, analysing game plays, developing plans and drilling the players together until moves become routine. Development is focused on the sub-groups that will put each tactic into practice. In basketball, the coach or manager has the role of integrating the team so that they collaborate instinctively in exactly the right manner, without getting in each other's way. The focus of development is with the team as a whole and applies to both social and technical integration.

Choosing the wrong model as the basis of a management approach would have dire consequences for the sports team. Similarly, choosing the wrong sports metaphor to apply to the business team may damage its ability to deliver. Sales teams may have most in common with a baseball team; an assembly line with American football; and a cross-functional project team with basketball.

An appropriate analogy can help the coach or manager work out how hands-on they need to be, how closely they should focus on the interdependencies between individuals and sub-groups, and how much emphasis to put on individual, group or team development. Using the sports analogy *well* can be very revealing in terms of building cooperation, understanding the importance of hand-offs between tasks, and strategic human resource management.

However, all analogies are only partial comparisons. Nancy Katz of Harvard Business School has looked in depth at the pluses and minuses of following the sports analogy. She concludes that common mistakes, in addition to choosing the wrong sports model, include:

- **Confusing coaching with managing**. Although coaching is important, it has less impact on the team than getting the structural variables right (e.g. the design of the task, the team itself and getting the required resources).

- **Building boundaries instead of bridges**. Not everyone responds well to a sporting analogy, and many can be turned off. A US-based conference organization had as its keynote speaker a locally famous sports coach, who made the assumption that the audience would understand the analogies to aspects of his sport (I'm not clear which game it was). Unfortunately, much of the audience was from outside the US and found the entire speech incomprehensible!

- **Assuming that winning is the only thing**. In business, there are many, much wider ethical issues to consider. Promoting a "winning is all" philosophy can be very dangerous. Katz quotes researcher Joshua Margolis,[6] whose work suggests that managers who overuse the sporting analogy can infer that "the workplace is ethically no more complex than the playing field".

Similarly, the analogy between an orchestra and a team has only limited validity. The analogy was first widely promoted by Peter Drucker, leading a number of prominent conductors to develop a profitable sideline in demonstrating teamwork to participants at management conferences. It has found its most fervent support in the metaphor of the jazz band.

Mary Hatch and Karl Weick make a passionate case for the jazz metaphor, based primarily on the fact that both demand constant improvisation and attention to the activities, strengths and skills of other team members. The strength of the jazz metaphor, they say, lies in its "exposition of improvisation and resilience as an alternative to planning and anticipating". Of course, structure and process are important to commercial success and progress, but only up to a point. In a study I conducted a few years ago into maverick companies,[7] I found a number of very successful organizations, including Wow Toys and Ben & Jerry's, which abjured formal business planning in favour of a constant learning dialogue with their customers. In general, the more comprehensive systems become, the less agile people can be in their responses to changing needs. When plans go wrong, as they will, a critical factor in performance is the speed the team shows in recognizing and reacting to the problem, and the resilience it demonstrates in dusting itself off and seeking a new way forward.

The limitations of the metaphor include the fact that, as Hatch and Weick subsequently discuss, "jazz musicians develop their music onstage through a set of musical interactions targeted toward one another rather than toward the audience".[8] The group becomes a vehicle for self-indulgence. There are work groups that have this characteristic (for example legal practices with many prima donnas), but it is debatable whether these ever become teams! Moreover, teams operate at very different levels of interdependence.

Various researchers into team dynamics have developed very different ways of classifying team types. Hackman[9] bases his typology on who (the leader/manager or the team members) takes responsibility for what. Team members always take responsibility for executing the task, but may or may not do so for monitoring and managing performance processes, designing the way the group functions, or designing how the group fits and interfaces with the wider organization. In **manager-led** teams, the manager decides what the goals are and how the team is structured; he or she also oversees the performance of the team. The manager controls the process, the selection of members and interactions outside the team. In **self-managing teams**, the manager retains responsibility for the goals and the context in which the team operates, but the team members manage the process. **Self-designing teams** go one step further and take responsibility for setting their own objectives. The manager provides resources and protection from the outside world. Finally, **self-governing teams** take responsibility in addition for designing the organizational context – not just what shall we do, but why are we doing it? Boards of directors are typical of this kind of team.

The usefulness of this kind of classification depends on two criteria: how easy it is to distinguish between team types and how clearly we can relate each to different situations. On the first criterion, this method of differentiation between team types is problematic. Teams may exhibit characteristics of more than one type, depending on the tasks they have been set.

In a previous study, I identified a hierarchy of task types based on the degree to which the manager or organization could safely delegate responsibility.[10] The "hierarchy of discretion" ranges from the fully prescriptive process (for example a telesales person working to a precise script) to self-defining work teams, which define both what they do and how they do it within their own frames of reference. Factors in determining the level of self-management exercised by the team include:

- Their expertise, as perceived by influential outsiders.
- The degree of risk involved (the higher the perceived risk, the higher the required controls).
- The level of innovation or independent thinking required (the more innovation required, the more discretion granted).
- Their track record in handling lesser risks.
- The balance of emphasis between process control and outcomes control. High process control combined with low outcomes control may often be seen in bureaucratic systems such as benefits payments, where the intended beneficiaries often miss or have to wait for their entitlements because the rules need to be followed. High outcomes control and low process control may argue for a much higher level of discretion and delegation. Low need for control of both is a rare situation, sometimes found for example in a university fundamental research environment, where outcomes are uncertain and process experimentation is an expected part of the task. High need for control of both process and outcomes may, paradoxically, argue for both a high degree of participation in the design of systems and a high degree of manager-led monitoring.

As the environment changes and the capabilities and experience of the team evolve, the distribution of responsibilities may have to change as well. Hackman's team types therefore should not be seen as bounded classifications, but as points on a changing spectrum.

On the second criterion – how clearly we can relate the team types to specific situations – we can be more positive. Table 2.1 overleaf shows some of the pluses and minuses of each team type.

Another view of team types comes from Edmondson,[11] who sees Hackman's classification as just one of three spectra on which teams may sit. These are:

- cross-function—single-function
- time-limited—enduring
- manager-led—self-led

TABLE 2.1

HACKMAN'S TEAM TYPES

TEAM TYPE	ADVANTAGES	DISADVANTAGES	BEST FOR...
Manager-led	Easy and cost-effective to start Clarity of task Clarity of responsibility	Manager may be over-extended Processes are not questioned Goals may not be understood/shared	Straightforward tasks, with high clarity of role and goal High-risk situations
Self-managing	Commitment Motivation/ morale Creativity	Harder to assess progress More time needed for discussion	Distributed operations, where each team has a geographical area or a discrete market and is relatively independent of other teams
Self-designing	Commitment Motivation/ morale Creativity	Hard to assess progress More opportunity for conflict Potentially less clarity about responsibilities Legitimacy	Complex, ill-defined or ambiguous problems "Blue-skies" development
Self-governing	Independence of operation and thinking	May become self-perpetuating Lack of checks and balances	Investigating serious problems (e.g. MRSA in hospitals)

The dynamics of the team depend on the combination of these dimensions. So a simple manufacturing assembly team might be semi-permanent, but operating with a high degree of autonomy.

One such team I observed some years ago made mirrors for motor vehicles. They had full control of the operation of their machinery, the planning of how they worked and – most importantly for them – how long and when they worked. They had responsibility for the quality of their production (although other, less autonomous teams made a point of impromptu, unofficial checks), but did not set their own production targets. Although they worked much shorter hours than a control group of teams operating under a manager-led style, their performance was higher on all measures of productivity, quality and customer service.

A different team might consist of people drawn from a variety of other teams to manage a short-term, urgent project, and be led in a relatively hands-on manner by a manager who understands the requirements in detail and recognizes that there is insufficient time to bring other team members up to the level of knowledge that would allow for a more autonomous approach.

Yet another typology bases its analysis on the flow of work within the team. The fourfold classification from Richard Ratliff and his colleagues[12] is:

- **Simple team**. These consist of a number of people carrying out basically the same task to achieve a large volume of output, for example the tellers counting the votes in an election, or an assembly operation where each operator constructs the same multi-component part.
- **Relay team**. Here "a sequence of tasks must be performed on an object (good or service), in a specified order", with the object passing from one person to another in sequence. Examples include making sandwiches at McDonald's and long-distance mail delivery.
- **Integrative work team**. These "combine a variety of related tasks to produce a product [with] several tasks performed at the same time". Examples include a hospital theatre team and book production.
- **Problem-solving team**. Here a variety of skills and knowledge are combined to tackle problems whose structure, boundaries and sometimes even definition may not be clear.

Team size

An analysis such as Ratliff's can be very helpful in determining appropriate team size, as Table 2.2 indicates.

TABLE 2.2

CALCULATING APPROPRIATE TEAM SIZE

TEAM TYPE	SIZE CALCULATION
Simple work team	Based on: • amount of work • time available to do it • how much work one person can do in the time available
Relay team	Based on: • amount of differentiation between sequential tasks • balancing of task assignments to avoid bottlenecks and idle resources • cycle time required
Integrated work team	Based on: • differentiation between tasks • "takt" time – productive time available divided by volume required
Problem-solving team	Based on: • "number of dimensions of the problem significantly affecting the solution"

Other factors that affect team size include:

◆ **Whether there is a need for reserve members**. Fire crew, for example, typically have a reserve capacity, both within each team and as back-up teams, to cope with serious emergencies.

- **Technological capabilities required**. These refer to the practical limits of doing the task. Ratliff and his colleagues use the example of an operating theatre, where cramped space and the need for instant communication limit the numbers present and the ability to give attention restricts the number of people who can participate through remote technology, giving advice.
- **Social needs**, concerning how people relate emotionally and psychologically to the team. Beyond a certain size, people find it difficult to retain familiarity with each other, in terms of both who they are and what their role is; as a result, their sense of personal identity with the team reduces. Ratliff's research suggests that the comfortable limit for a simple team is 15, for integrated teams between 5 and 8, and for problem-solving teams up to 10 people. It proved more difficult to define an ideal maximum size for relay teams, which ranged from as few as 2 or 3 people to as many as 24. From a practical perspective, people's needs to form comfortably sized social groups will lead them to create sub-groups within a work group that is too large, and this can be either positive or negative for team cohesion and performance, depending on how each clique sees its relationship with the others.

Other research on team size[13] tells us that the bigger the group:

- The less satisfied the members feel with it
- The lower the productivity
- The greater the propensity to experience "social loafing" – a decrease in individual effort, based on the expectation that others will pick up the slack. A seminal experiment by a French engineer with teams pulling heavy loads found that the average amount of effort exerted by an individual alone was slightly more than twice that of the effort of the same individuals when working in teams of eight.[14]

The value of multiple perspectives

What do all these different ways of looking at teams tell us, apart from the fact that there is no one, simple way of differentiating between teams? First, whether a team really is a team is a very useful starting point for working out what kinds of approaches are needed, what learning the team will have to acquire or – as is quite often the case – whether the group needs to reassess whether it wants or needs to be a team anyway. It is quite possible, especially at the top of large organizations, for a group or several complementary groups to lead successfully.[15] Indeed, the structure of company boards is often designed to prevent executives and non-executives becoming too cosy.

Secondly, the more perspectives that a team, or an external facilitator or a coach working with a team, can apply to understand the dynamics of how it functions, the wider the range of solutions it can generate to tackle performance problems. Thirdly, diversity of perspective is in itself a fertile source for learning dialogue.

The checklist below is a useful summary for helping a group decide whether or not it is a team.

- To what extent are we agreed on:
    - What the key goals are?
    - What the priorities are?
- How dependent are we on each other for achieving our individual goals?
- How dependent are we on each other for achieving the collective goal?
- How adaptable are we in the roles we play?
- Do we *feel* more like a group or more like a team?
- Do our direct reports see us as a group or as a team?
- Are we willing to give up personal priorities for the common team goals?

What makes a team effective?

Given the association of coaching with performance, what makes a team effective is a fundamental question. Individual performance is usually measured through a mixture of "hard" targets, such as meeting sales objectives, and "soft" targets, such as being supportive to colleagues. A common principle is that there should always be an element of improvement in some or all of these objectives – standing still is not acceptable. Team performance is similarly measured on achievement of a mixture of hard and soft targets, for example production costs and quality (although quality can often be expressed through both hard and soft measures).

In this section, we explore a range of topics that relate to team performance. In particular, we consider the impact on performance of:

◆ How diverse the team members are
◆ Creativity and work standardization
◆ Communication within and outside the team
◆ How the team handles conflict
◆ Team leadership
◆ The quality of teamwork

Diverse or similar: Which is best?

Several studies have found that top management teams that have diverse backgrounds and capabilities make more innovative, higher-quality decisions than those that are relatively homogeneous.[16]

Being diverse isn't enough, however. Using diversity effectively in decision making demands that the team has processes that allow its members to have open and positively critical dialogue, to investigate issues with an open mind and to be willing to learn from the situation and from each other. They also need to be able to identify and understand others' perspectives and synthesize these into a decision that is better than that which might have emerged through the horse-trading and compromise that so often characterize management decision making. Effective decision-making dialogue is rigorous, structured and synthesizing; that is, it pulls together multiple threads and perspectives to create wider choices and more accurate evaluation of risks and benefits.[17]

However, high-quality decision making is valueless unless it is supported by consensus among team members with regard to what the decision means and the commitments that will be needed both individually and jointly. The development of understanding and commitment need to occur while the decision is being made.[18] Both seem to depend to a significant extent on the quality of the dialogue within the team – in particular, the variety of different perspectives considered and the willingness to adapt and amalgamate these.

Diversity comes in many forms. Those that have been investigated extensively in terms of team effectiveness relate to culture, expertise and gender.

Cultural diversity

Some of the most interesting studies of team diversity have examined transnational teams.[19] Geography and culture ensure that such teams start with built-in potential for conflict. In particular, it may take longer to build shared meaning systems and a sense of collective team identification. Shared meaning systems relate to the interpretations that members place on words and actions, and the filters they apply in evaluating situations and other people's behaviour. Researchers sometimes talk of having a team mental model, which they define as a "shared psychological representation of a team's environment constructed to permit sense-making and guide appropriate group action".[20] Collective team identification is the emotional significance that members of the group attach to their membership of that group. Other factors that may play a part in collective team identification include knowing that they are part of the group and the value they attach to membership. It is the emotional significance that determines the motivational force.[21]

As transnational teams gradually learn to work together, those that are successful create hybrid cultures over time. This emergent culture is the basis for a common sense of identity within the group, which allows team members to evaluate their performance, makes it easier for them to work together and increases the quality of what they do.

Christopher Early and Elaine Mosakowski[22] examined the performance of teams with high, moderate and low cultural diversity. The highly homogeneous teams were those where members saw each other as "like themselves" and had similar collective expectations about roles, norms and behaviours. Highly heterogeneous teams had very different perceptions and expectations; and moderately heterogeneous teams were in between.

Their study confirmed the broad conclusion that homogeneity encourages affinity for the team and its members, while heterogeneity encourages creativity. However, it also confirmed that moderately heterogeneous teams were the least effective, being outperformed by teams that were composed of people who saw themselves as different, and by teams where there was a high degree of perceived homogeneity. Moderate diversity, it seems, encourages people to break into sub-groups, based on real or imagined attributes or interests. When the team meets threats or challenges, its members retreat into their sub-groups, which are effectively faultlines within team cohesion, and this stimulates relational conflict.

Teams that have a unified culture tend to outperform those that don't, because they have better communication and coordination between members. However, Early and Mosakowski found that highly heterogeneous teams, having few pre-existing bases for forming sub-groups or a collective identity, often develop a hybrid culture that reflects the diversity of the members, without losing the potential for creativity. Developing this culture required a number of things to happen. The team needed to develop rules for interpersonal and task-related interactions, a high level of shared expectations about the performance expected, effective styles of communication and conflict management, and a common identity.

It may well be that the need to establish role and task clarity obliges the team to engage in open dialogue, and that fosters the building of trust and shared understanding and identity.

So, while cultural diversity in the team is often dysfunctional at the beginning, those teams that capitalize on the differences and develop a common identity eventually become as effective as those that begin with high homogeneity – and have some built-in advantages, in terms of potential for innovating.

Expertise diversity

This is the extent of difference or specialization in the knowledge and skills that members of a team bring to the task. It can easily lead to conflict, with individuals and groups defending the integrity or superiority of their own knowledge base. (The world of executive coaching is a superb current example of this!)

Gender mix

A team's gender mix can have significant effects on how it approaches its tasks. The differences in performance appear to relate to two factors, according to research into all-male and all-female groups: tasks or environments that favour the interests or abilities of one gender over the other; and differences in how men and women behave in groups. For example, "the tendency for men in groups to offer opinions and suggestions, and the tendency of women to act friendly and agree with others".[23]

THE PERFORMANCE BENEFITS OF DIVERSITY

Although having multiple perspectives on issues may sometimes be uncomfortable and lead to conflict, it also helps avoid groupthink, when individual opinion is submerged to conform with the group. In general, groups make more extreme judgements than do individuals. Part of the reason is that when people are asked to make judgements outside of the context of a group, their sense of self-identity dominates their choices. Yet when they are in a group situation, the mores of the group predominate as they try to live up to their social identity.

Either people change their own opinion to conform with the group norm, or they are swung by the quality of the arguments. In practice, both factors play a part. Where the issue is clear cut and the choices unambiguous, the persuasion of the argument dominates the shift of opinion; the greater the ambiguity, the more people are influenced by the instinct to conform socially.[24]

Creativity and work standardization

At first sight, creativity and work standardization appear antipathetical. Companies place high value on teams that innovate and experiment with new ways of managing their work.[25] In theory at least, teams that are more innovative are more flexible in their response to change, more resilient and have higher performance.[26] Establishing and maintaining a creative team environment ("one in which members encourage each other to engage in creative activities and to employ creative work processes"[27]) is a priority not just in the "creative" sectors, such as the arts and media, but also in any environment where adaptation to changed circumstances is needed.

Bureaucratic procedures stifle creativity. Yet standards and routines are important for maintaining levels of service.[28] Customers like to know what to expect in the services and products they buy. Many tasks, such as infection prevention in hospitals, aircraft maintenance or emergency procedures, have to be carried out "by the book" because variation from the standard may have dire consequences.

Therefore, while both creativity and standardization improve team effectiveness, their underlying mechanisms appear to work against each other. However, recent studies suggest a more complex dynamic.[29] Whereas customer satisfaction is strongly associated with work standardization, overall team performance seems to be more strongly associated with creativity. When the team is responding to

change, one of the results of experimentation is to unsettle customers, reducing perceived service quality. Being creative also
requires more time, which may be taken from the customer interface.
But if the team does not innovate, its service offering may be over-
taken by market changes, leading again to customer dissatisfaction.

The trick is to find ways that allow teams to innovate, but to
contain the negative fall-out from doing so, while maintaining standard processes and routines where it is most important. Two complementary tactics appear to work reasonably well: innovating in
small, contained areas, one at a time, while constantly monitoring
the impact of changes; and focusing on the whole system, to ensure
that changes in one area don't have unexpected dysfunctional effects
in others.

Contrary to expectation, giving teams greater freedom to manage their own affairs doesn't necessarily lead to higher creativity.
According to a study by James Barker,[30] when a team becomes self-
managing it can impose value-based norms and rules that are even
more constrictive than before – and hence be less creative.

Among questions coaches may ask to help the team consider
these issues are:

◆ What response does each situation demand?
◆ Do we have the habit of innovating and the information to do
    so without affecting customer satisfaction?

A related issue here is the way in which the work is structured. We
have already touched on the reality that teams don't always deliver
more than individuals working on their own. Ruth Wageman's
studies of groups with different levels of interdependence[31] indicate
that teams perform best when their tasks and outcomes are organized to be either highly interdependent (working closely together
and reliant on each other) or highly independent (individuals working largely on their own). Hybrid groups perform quite poorly and
have both low-quality interaction processes and low member
satisfaction.

Communication

Communication within the team is helped by having clear goals and clearly defined roles, responsibilities and task structures. Clarity of goals and structures also reduces conflict and promotes the development of "shared mental models"[32] – common views of the work and the environment in which the team operates – that make communication between team members easier.

In general, the higher the interdependence of the team, the greater the need for frequent communication. Teams need both transactional communication (information and guidance about tasks and processes) and relational information (for developing shared understanding, building trust and maintaining social cohesion).

Communication with the world outside the team was explored by Deborah Ancona and her colleagues in the late 1980s and early 1990s.[33] In one study of five consulting firms, they identified three strategies that teams and their leaders adopted to manage the relationships with people outside the team:

◆ **Informing** – remaining relatively isolated from the environment while the team worked out what it wanted to do, before revealing its intentions.
◆ **Parading** – high levels of passive observation of the environment and internal team building, fostering visibility by keeping outsiders up to date on progress within the team.
◆ **Probing** – finding out about the external environment by interacting with it, consulting outsiders, carrying out experiments with them and actively promoting what the team had achieved.

Probing teams were rated most highly in performance by outsiders, although member satisfaction and cohesiveness suffered in the short run. It seems that effective teams develop strategies to alleviate the downsides of this externally focused approach.

In a later study of 38 new product development teams with David Caldwell,[34] Ancona observed that teams engage in vertical communication aimed at moulding the views of top management (the **ambassadorial** role), horizontal communication aimed at coordinating work and obtaining feedback (the **task-coordinating** role), and horizontal communication aimed at **general scanning** of the technical and market environment. In this case, they found that ambassadorial activities were more associated with positive rating of team performance by top management (in terms of budgets and adherence to schedules) early in the team's life. But as the teams matured, task-coordinator activities were more positively related to top management's view of how innovative the team was. General scanning was related to low ratings by top management at both times.

Among the conclusions that can be drawn from this study is that teams need to be proactive in adapting their strategies in communicating with the outside. A simple tool I have used with teams to surface such communication issues is the matrix in Figure 2.1.

FIGURE 2.1

COMMUNICATION PERSPECTIVES

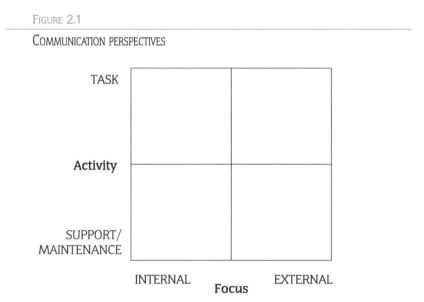

The coaching dialogue in this respect begins by identifying the needs for communication both within the team and outside it, under a number of headings – information, coordination, reputation management, autonomy, resource access and so on – for both the primary tasks of the team and the activities it has to undertake in support of task delivery, such as taking time out for learning. It then moves to how well the team manages each of these communication needs and what feedback methods are in place to determine whether the communication processes are working. A critical issue here is whether people want or need to be informed, consulted or involved in decision making in each of these areas. Finally, the coaching dialogue explores how the team can improve its overall communication and which areas should be prioritized for improvement.

Conflict

Conflict within a team is bad, isn't it? Not necessarily. It depends on the type of conflict and the context in which the team operates.

Researchers identify three distinct types of conflict. **Relationship conflict** – where people have interpersonal problems, personality clashes, or real or imagined grievances with other members of the team – is almost always damaging to performance. Relationship conflict contributes to stress, increases turnover of membership and reduces people's ability to think clearly, especially when they are managing complex information. People engaged in relationship conflict often respond by withdrawing (physically, psychologically or both) from the situation.[35] Communication is reduced if people try to pretend the problem isn't there.

Relationship conflict affects performance negatively in three ways[36]:

◆ People lose the ability to deal rationally with information provided to them.
◆ They stop listening and put up barriers to ideas from people they don't like or who annoy them.
◆ They divert energy to discussing, resolving or ignoring issues relating to the conflict.

Task conflict, in contrast, may have either positive or negative effects on performance. On the negative side, most people dislike being questioned critically about their ideas or what they do. Even a positive performance evaluation can create negative feelings, because the process of critical analysis is uncomfortable and feels threatening.[37] People in teams where there is a strong consensus about how tasks should be done tend to have higher job satisfaction and more commitment to staying in the team.[38]

Research in recent years confirms that whether task conflict is beneficial or damaging depends on the nature of the task itself. The simpler and more routine the task, the more consistently negative the impact of conflict about it. The more complex and uncertain the task, the more opportunity there is to use different perspectives to come to better decisions and improve processes. Benefits of positively managed task conflict include:

- Avoiding groupthink, through critical evaluation[39] and better decisions overall.[40]
- Greater creativity – teams often feel pressure to achieve consensus and will not consider innovative ideas unless there is an element of conflict.[41]
- Better identification and understanding of the issues involved.[42]
- Better task completion, use of resources and customer service.[43]

When conflict comes out into the open, it may not always be obvious whether it is a task or relationship issue. Task conflict can cause frustration that spills over into relationship conflict and vice versa. Bringing relationship conflict to the surface for open discussion and resolution in the group context may not always be beneficial. A study of successful string quartets,[44] for example, found that a strategy of compromises, such as taking turns, avoidance of open discussion about personality clashes and staying focused on the task, was productive. In this context, discussion of task conflict can be seen as a means of coping indirectly with relationship conflict. It may be that relationship conflict, being felt individually, is best managed at an individual level.

Teasing out the underlying cause and type of conflict is a key role for the coach, which we will explore in Chapter 5. It helps if teams have a set of norms about when and how conflict is aired. These might include specific forums, such as team meetings, and agreed methods of presenting a conflict so that dialogue begins with an acceptance that both parties are approaching the issue and each other with goodwill.

Rules a team might adopt for managing conflict

Occasional conflict within a work team is inevitable. We can choose whether or not we use it to mutual advantage, but good teamwork demands the latter. To that end we will:

- Reflect on conflict situations to clarify them in our own minds before bringing them for discussion

- Always attempt to resolve conflict first with the individuals concerned; secondly, if required, at a team meeting

- Accept that the other party has a different perspective, which may be based on different priorities and expectations

- Seek to understand the other party's perspective

- Seek solutions that meet both parties' requirements and support the goals of the team

- Commit and stick to solutions agreed

However, having norms relating to open discussion of conflict does not necessarily mean that conflict will be better handled. One study[45] found that "while such norms were associated with an increase in the number and intensity of relationship conflicts, they did not increase members' ability to deal with the conflicts constructively" –

in other words, just bringing issues to the surface isn't going to help unless team members have the skills to manage conflict effectively. Again, this is an important issue for the team coach, whose role is not to solve team conflict but to help people develop the competence to resolve conflict for themselves.

More recently, a third type of conflict has been identified and explored. **Process conflict** relates to decisions about allocating duties and resources, for example who should do what and how much responsibility each should have. This kind of conflict is associated with lower group morale and productivity[46] – the result of arguing between team members. However, like task conflict, it can be beneficial in certain circumstances, such as when the group is deciding how it will tackle its task.[47]

A study of team performance and types of conflict found that teams that performed well were characterized by low but increasing levels of process conflict, low levels of relationship conflict (which rose slightly near project deadlines) and moderate levels of task conflict, concentrated at the mid point of a project. Members of teams with this ideal profile tended to have shared value systems before they joined. They demonstrated high levels of trust and respect and discussed conflict openly, particularly around the project mid point.[48]

It is a paradox that conflict seems to improve the quality of decision making, by ensuring that different perspectives are considered, but weakens the ability of team members to work together.[49] Effective teams have to maintain a delicate balance between having enough difference to maintain a reasonably high level of conflict of ideas, but not so much that the team descends into relationship conflict.

Rather than reduce the level of difference to accommodate the risks of relationship conflict, teams may be better off attempting to raise their resilience to diversity, perhaps through various forms of diversity awareness and building the skills of diversity dialogue. Figure 2.2 is a useful device for helping the coach open out a learning conversation about where the team wants and needs to be in terms of managing conflict.

FIGURE 2.2

DIVERSITY AND CONFLICT

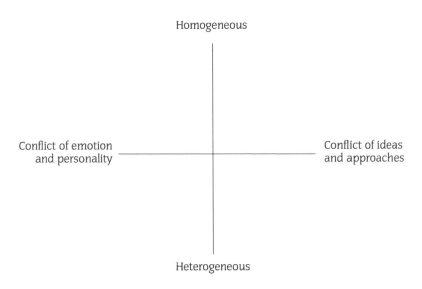

Role of the leader

It is fascinating that much of the literature on team functioning in recent years has ignored the role of the leader. This is not a book about leadership, although we shall from time to time be drawn into aspects of the topic. Suffice it at this point to say that there are at least four major themes of relevance here:

◈ **What team leaders do and don't do that affects the team's performance**. Elements of this include the leader's ability and behaviour in negotiating with the outside world and protecting the team from it, developing the skills of the team, motivating, clarifying goals, being an appropriate role model, and generally creating and maintaining the environment in which the team can succeed.

◈ **The interplay in all effective teams between formal and informal leadership**. Although it is possible for some types of team to flourish by constantly looking to a formal leader for instruction and guidance, in most cases the effectiveness of the team depends to a considerable extent on individual team members exerting leadership in circumstances where they have particular knowledge, skills or plain interest.

- **The concept of followership** – the ability to respond to and stimulate good leadership in others. The title of Alistair Mant's seminal book on leadership, *The Leaders You Deserve*,[50] expresses the point well. Proactive team membership demands that people exert effort not only in fulfilling their part of the collective task, but in ensuring that their colleagues are able to do the same – including the leader. Effective leaders both encourage and welcome this support from their team members.

- **How people attribute success and failure within teams**. "Attributional bias" refers to the phenomenon by which people misassign responsibility for performance. Studies show that team members tend to assign a disproportionate share of the credit for team successes to leaders or to "star performers", and a disproportionate share of the blame for team failures to internal scapegoats.[51]

The interaction between the team and the team leader is fertile ground for coaching, from the perspective of both the leader and the other team members. Some of the questions that stimulate thinking and behaviour change in the team leader are:

- What is the quality of your relationship with the team?
- Do you respect the team and do they respect you?
- Do you and the team share the same goals? How do you know?
- Does the team understand your needs for information, learning and upward support?
- What does the team need you for?
- What is the appropriate balance for this team in your managing upwards and downwards?
- What issues do you and the team avoid discussing?
- What decisions and actions do you most often procrastinate about?

- What could you stop doing that would improve the team's performance?
- What could you do more of that would improve the team's performance?
- How much leadership does this team require?
- What style of leadership would be most appropriate?
- If you could choose your dream team, what would it be like?
- What could you do to turn your existing team into the dream team?

Asking the same questions from the perspective of the team itself gives the coach an opportunity to compare and contrast and to explore at a fundamental level how the team functions and what prevents it working optimally.

Who selects the leader may also be an issue. An experiment comparing the performance of teams where the leaders were appointed with teams that selected their own leaders found that the latter performed better. The explanation seems to have to do with a difference in the attitudes adopted by the two types of leader: those who were appointed were more likely to feel superior and therefore more likely to assert themselves at the expense of team identity.[52] In a similar vein, an experiment by Dunchurch College training centre found that teams where the managers explained the task and made themselves available, but gave no orders, outperformed those managed in a consultative style, which in turn outperformed those working in a command-and-control style.

The implications for teams include that the style of leadership should be negotiated between the leader and the members, that leadership effectiveness should be a topic for open dialogue within the team, and that leaders should pay at least as much attention to how they relate to their direct reports as to how they relate to their bosses. These are all, of course, fertile topics for a coaching conversation, given the reluctance of many leaders and their teams to address them of their own volition.

Teamwork

Teamwork is one of those words that everyone recognizes but is difficult to define. Working *in* a team does not necessarily equate to working *as* a team. Collaboration comes in many shades of willingness, commitment, efficiency and effectiveness. A more pragmatic construct is teamwork quality,[53] which covers the wide range of task and behavioural interactions inherent in well-managed collaboration.

Teamwork quality involves six components:

◆ **Communication** – communication that supports teamwork is appropriately frequent, formalized, structured and open. The word *appropriately* is important here. Different team tasks and different team structures require different levels of each of these aspects. Fixed routine and meetings with tight agendas are important for making decisions and reviewing operations; *ad hoc* meetings in the corridor or informal exchanges online are important for building relationship quality and bouncing ideas around. Open conversation about behaviours, although generally preferable, may sometimes need to give way to circumspection, while the team focuses on an urgent activity and until the situation is more conducive to introspection and brutal honesty.

◆ **Coordination** – coordination concerns the level of common understanding about how and what each member is contributing, and the interrelationship between their contributions. Clear goals and priorities are integral to this.

◆ **Balance of member contributions** – everyone in the team is able and does give the full benefit of their knowledge and experience; dominant individuals do not suppress the ideas and views of others.

◆ **Mutual support** – having a cooperative rather than a competitive frame of mind; showing mutual respect, giving assistance and developing other people's ideas.

◆ **Effort** – having positive norms about sharing workloads and giving the team task priority over other obligations.

- **Cohesion** – "sticking together" – seems to consist of three elements: how well team members like and get on with each other, how committed they are to the team task, and how proud they feel to be part of this group (sometimes called team spirit).[54]

SOCIAL IDENTITY

One of the critical identifiers of a team is the strength of its collective social identity. Research into social identity theory, which says that people are what salient others expect them to be, reveals some interesting clues as to what is happening when people feel they belong to a team:

- Teams that foster interdependence and interaction between members use "us" and "we" a lot more than "I" and "me".[55]

- Teams develop their own shared myths, symbols, social roles and ways of interpreting the world around them – they provide support for attitudes or behaviours of which people outside the team might disapprove.

- Self-identity and team identity are rarely more than an uneasy compromise. Research into induction of new recruits into work teams shows that recognizing and managing this collectively at the early stages of team membership increases job satisfaction and reduces work–family conflict.[56] (The family, of course, provides a powerful alternative source of self-identity.)

- Scapegoats emerge internally and externally. Scapegoating within the team may reinforce norms of behaviour, but it can be highly stressful and leave people afraid to step out of line or admit problems, in case it is their turn next. Scapegoating directed towards others outside the team can in certain circumstances enhance cohesion in terms of team solidarity and consistency[57]: conflict that would have arisen between team members is projected instead on outsiders. Addressing these protective delusions through open exploration of individual and group feelings reduces the need for people to rely on scapegoating.[58]

A comprehensive overview of the knowledge, skills and ability (KSAs) necessary for teamwork identifies three interpersonal KSAs and two self-management KSAs. The interpersonal ones are:

- **Conflict resolution** – recognizing potential for conflict and managing it to achieve win–win outcomes.
- **Collaborative problem solving** – knowing when and how to solve problems together.
- **Communication** – understanding and using networks, communicating openly and supportively, listening effectively, communicating non-verbally and communicating socially.

The self-management KSAs are:

- **Goal setting and performance management** – establishing specific, challenging and accepted team goals; monitoring and giving feedback.
- **Planning and task coordination** – coordinating and synthesizing activities, information and interdependencies between members; balancing workload; and managing task and role expectations within the team.

How teams evolve

Teams obviously change over time, and it is helpful for the coach to have some idea of where in its evolution a particular team sits.

The rubric of forming, storming, norming, performing and adjourning[59] in the development of new teams was proposed in the mid-1960s. Forming stages, where the group comes together, were marked by courtesy, confusion and caution; storming by concern, conflict and criticism; norming by cooperation, collaboration, cohesion and commitment; performing by challenge, creativity and consideration of each other; and adjourning by compromise, communication, consensus and closure.

The concept and language of this description are neat, but don't necessarily depict what actually happens. Such tidy, logical, clear-cut phases don't usually happen in the real world.

Studies by Connie Gersick[60] in the late 1980s show a very different dynamic to how teams evolve. She focused on project teams in a variety of organizations and observed how they behaved over time (ranging from a few days to months). What she found was that, irrespective of the length of time the team existed, it went through a similar dynamic, which consisted of:

◆ A distinctive approach to the task, which emerged very rapidly as soon as the team came together.

◆ A period of inertia, where nothing much changed in the way its members worked.

◆ A sudden period of transition, at the half-way point of the team life cycle, in which "in a concentrated burst of activity, groups dropped old patterns, reengaged with their outside supervisors, adopted new perspectives on their work, and made dramatic progress... a new approach to [the] task".

◆ A second period of inertia, while they executed the plans made during the transition.

◆ A final burst of activity, amounting to a second transition, to finish the work – "groups made one last change in their behaviour patterns, just before their deadlines".

Gersick describes this process as a punctuated equilibrium. The collective action at the mid point seems to occur because this is a psychological marker point, at which most of the group will have at least begun to reflect on what is going well and less well. If the mid point passes without collective reflection, "a team will experience the passing as a failure and shared sense of opportunity will probably be lost until the next temporal milestone". Timely intervention by a coach is one way to ensure that this doesn't happen.

None of this helps us a great deal when it comes to those teams that are semi-permanent (stable). There is an assumption in most of the academic research that teams will remain essentially the same in task and membership; or perhaps this is simply a reflection of the fact that it's a lot easier to study teams that don't change. From one perspective, each time someone leaves and/or is replaced, it is a different team. However, the group norms, tasks and procedures may remain the same. We don't have a valid model of what happens to these teams over time, but some relevant observations are that the longer the team exists:

♦ The less willing the members may be to challenge group norms.
♦ The less aware they become of the external world.
♦ The greater the likelihood that they will bury relationship conflict, or that, conversely, it will turn into open warfare.
♦ The more difficult it becomes for newcomers to become socialized (i.e. to fit in).

The coach's repertoire

It should be evident by now that teams are highly complex social entities, that the influences on their performance are even more complex, and that there are no simple answers or approaches when working with teams. Improving individual performance does not necessarily improve team performance. The effective team coach therefore needs a wide repertoire of flexible responses that equip them to help the team deal with any or all of the issues of team dynamics reviewed in this chapter. Frequently several of these dynamics may be in play at the same time, so the team coach needs to be able to recognize them, untangle them and help the team devise coherent and integrated strategies to manage the complexity. We shall examine some of these responses in Chapters 3, 4 and 5. Moreover, as we shall see in Chapter 6, the coach's role also includes raising the team's awareness of its own dynamics – the influences on it and how it reacts to them – and helping the team become proficient at coaching itself.

FINAL COACHING QUESTION

Given how difficult and complex getting high performance out of a team can be, does this team have the collective energy and will to be high performing?

CHAPTER THREE

Coaching the team

"When the team is managed by coaching, the job gets done well and the team develops at the same time." | **Sir John Whitmore**[1]

There isn't a commonly accepted definition of team coaching, perhaps because teams differ so much in nature and purpose. The working definition that has evolved from our work with organizations and teams is:

Helping the team improve performance, and the processes by which performance is achieved, through reflection and dialogue.

It's not perfect, but it works for most teams.

Equally, there isn't a standard role definition for the team coach. In the examples overleaf, England rowing coach Jurgen Grobler is clearly describing a hands-on style of sports coaching very different from that of former England rugby coach Sir Clive Woodward – yet both are undeniably successful. Grobler's list is interesting because it emphasizes how demanding coaches must be of themselves if they expect great things from the team. It is unlikely in most business coaching situations that the reputation of the coach will be so intimately bound up with the team, but it can be very useful to view the relationship between coach performance and team performance as closely intertwined. The team coach's role is not passive or soft; it is both predictive and responsive, supportive and rigorous.

Jurgen Grobler's rules for team coaching

1 Show you love your job

2 Guard mutual trust and openness

3 Question yourself before you question the team

4 Don't run away from tough decisions

5 Deal with people as individuals, differently

6 No criticism means no progress

7 Listen to what your team is telling you

8 Shun favouritism

Team coaching on the rugby field

Sir Clive Woodward draws a clear distinction between the roles of individual and team coaches. In his squad, every player has an individual coach, who works with him on personal motivation and personal performance. Conflict or communication failure between players is managed by these coaches, who may work together to resolve interpersonal issues.

Sir Clive sees his role as team coach in terms of helping the team clarify and focus on the tasks they collectively want to achieve and on the process by which they will achieve those tasks (i.e. what they have to do to score multiple tries and/or drop goals each game).

This separation of role has clear benefits in the sporting context, but it demands a very high level of coaching resource. So the Woodward model can realistically only apply in business at the most senior levels. In the ordinary work team, where perhaps the only coach available is the team leader or at best a single external resource, the roles may have to be combined.

The business case for team coaching

Given the volume of recent research into the business benefits of coaching for individuals, it is surprising that there is so little hard evidence for the benefits of team coaching. What little empirical evidence there is, we examine later in this chapter. For the moment, let's focus on the anecdotal evidence and the critical issue of *making* the business case.

In making the business case to top management, there are only a few arguments that truly achieve both rational and emotional endorsement. These are, broadly:

◆ To improve some specific aspect(s) of performance (the more general, the less credible)
◆ To make things happen faster
◆ To make things happen differently

Improving performance

The primary reason for investing in team coaching is to improve team performance. The problem is that performance can mean many different things. Is it the volume of work output or the quality of output? The volume of sales or profit? The degree to which the team does its own work as planned or how well it supports the work of other teams? Customer growth or customer retention? How efficient it is or how effective?

The case for team coaching begins with the creative and motivated consideration of these and similar questions, which rarely get asked. In theory, establishing a team mission statement should help, but more often than not this becomes an excuse for *not* thinking about such issues on a regular, day-to-day basis. The problem is partly that whatever is decided about mission and priorities one day tends to change the next. High-performance teams don't waste their time and energy finding solid answers. Instead, they concentrate on making sure that they are asking the right questions, at the right time, so that they can keep abreast of shifting requirements.

In measuring performance, therefore, the team and those to whom it is accountable need to identify both flexible, current measures and the few underlying, permanent indicators.

GAINING A SENSE OF STABILITY

A sales team had grown punch drunk from frequent changes to the bonus system, which was constantly shifting to reflect changes in the company's desired customer mix, and from team to individual bonuses and back again. Through coaching dialogue, the team was able to recognize that the most important and durable aspect of its performance was the maintenance of margin on sales. The team members negotiated with senior management that this measure would be the core of the bonus scheme, worth 60 per cent of the whole. In addition, they would take on two other priorities on which to focus their performance, reviewing and if necessary changing them for other priorities once every six months.

This gave them a sense of stability to plan how to achieve performance targets and make the necessary adaptations in systems and behaviours. It also gave them space and opportunity to manage potentially conflicting performance priorities. For example, increasing customer volume could not be achieved without damaging margins, unless both existing and new customers were persuaded to switch to a high-value-added service.

Good coaching questions for improving performance are:

◆ How do other people judge your performance?
◆ Whose judgement matters (most)?

◆ What can you do to exert more control over how your performance is measured?

◆ What do you want to do about it?

Another recorded benefit of team coaching is that it improves the leader's ability to manage the performance of individuals. Managers generally are prone to misattribute the causes of poor performance. They tend to over-emphasize motivation and under-emphasize other factors – in particular, lack of knowledge or skill.[2] All of this reinforces the message that poor performance has a lot more to do with poor management and failure to coach than with unwillingness on the employee's part. Team coaching provides a forum where such misattributions can be identified, addressed and resolved.

Making things happen faster

New teams – particularly project teams and stable teams formed as a result of a merger or restructuring – are often expected to hit the ground running. The problem is that most new fields are full of rabbit holes, to stretch a metaphor. Coaching is arguably the only reliable means of ensuring that a team moves rapidly through the stages of development (see Chapter 2). Without coaching, each stage is likely to be prolonged by failures of communication, mistrust, inadequate processes and avoidance of the important but less obvious questions.

Making things happen differently

Culture change programmes have a dismal record of success, in spite of all the effort and money thrown at them. Part of the problem is that the change process typically misses several key ingredients. One of these is the opportunity to explore in depth people's concerns about the change and how they personally will learn to behave differently. Whirlwind campaign events do not create the environment for such considered reflection and introspection, either individually or for the team as a whole.

However, in my experience and observation, wherever culture change has been accompanied by a significant investment in individual and team coaching, the pace and depth of genuine change have been radically increased. Team coaching provides the wherewithal to understand the nature and impact of cultural change, to confront personal and team demons, to create and follow through pragmatic plans for making change happen, and to support people as they struggle with embedding new attitudes and behaviours.

In addition, there is some evidence that team coaching contributes to:

◆ Reducing conflict both within the team and between teams (the latter being one of top management's main headaches in many organizations)
◆ Increasing the efficiency of team processes and systems (by questioning why things are done the way they are)
◆ Improving the quality of team communication with key external stakeholders (again, in particular top management)
◆ Retention of valued employees (not least because people feel they are continuing to learn)
◆ Succession planning by raising the profile and promotability of the team leader/manager and of team members
◆ Knowledge management in general (because team members are able to use their coaching skills to help the learning of people outside the team)

In making the case for team coaching, the best approach is often to engage top management in a coaching dialogue. Useful questions include:

◆ Is this organization ready for team coaching?
◆ What are you relying on the team in question to do for the organization?

- What are the consequences if it doesn't deliver?
- How would you know if it didn't deliver?
- How much effort are you prepared to put in to make sure that it does deliver?
- What are the chances of it doing so *without* coaching?
- What has the pay-off for team coaching got to be to cover the investment costs of time and imported coaching expertise?
- How would you measure the pay-off?
- What are the risks, if any, of providing team coaching?

The complexities of team coaching

As we indicated in Chapter 1, the main difference between individual coaching and team coaching is that the latter is much more complex. Broadly the same themes occur as with individual coaching, but there are extra dimensions to consider. Among these are the following.

Confidentiality

An issue for individual coaching at the executive coaching level is how to maintain the confidentiality of what is said in the coaching sessions, yet enable the organization to feel that progress is being made on areas important for the client's performance. A general rule is that the existence of the relationship is public knowledge, but what is said within it is private. (There are always legal and ethical limits to the scope of confidentiality.) In team coaching, however, a different dynamic applies. The transparency of team discussions can be high between the team and the organization. Yet one-to-one conversations between the coach and individual members need to be held in relatively strict confidence, in order not to restrain the quality of team dialogue. It can be a very delicate balancing act for the coach to hold tight on information gained one to one, yet knowing that it is relevant to wider team conversations.

CREATING SYNERGY

When a Danish organization decided to focus more on management and leadership issues, teamwork among the nine-person top management group was a priority. The work of the organization involves daily pressure with tough deadlines, in a very political environment, where there is an emphasis on delivering highly professional services. The managing director wanted to combine the implementation of a 360-degree leader feedback tool with real and solid support to all the managers, including himself, to ensure learning and development.

An external executive coach, with experience as a process consultant, was engaged to work with the team. The programme included six individual coaching sessions for each manager over a period of almost a year with an interval of six to eight weeks between them, combined with team coaching in various forms approximately every two months. In addition, managers had the opportunity to buy more individual coaching if needed, and to do duo or trio coaching with relevant managers where they felt they had common challenges. Each manager also had the opportunity to use the coach as a facilitator in various workshops and meetings in their own department or management team. Many of these "extra" activities were used during the programme.

Team coaching was implemented in several ways, ranging from the coach participating in normal management team meetings to specific workshops of between half a day and two days in duration.

Everybody agreed on the ground rule of all individual coaching sessions being 100 per cent confidential; that is, no reporting back on individuals or units to the director. Equally important, all parties involved also agreed on a model where the coach collected what were called "main themes", "patterns" and general topics that popped up again and again during the individual coaching work. These main themes were given to everyone in writing and provided the main platform for the content of the team coaching.

Examples of "main themes" included:

- How do we ensure a better learning environment in our team?

- How do we use each other more as discussion partners in daily work life?

- Ensure more clarity on roles and responsibility between departments – also at employee level

- More feedback to and from the managing director as the team leader

- Clarifying the role of a specific department to the rest of the organization

- Reorganizing meeting structures and agendas

- Clarifying the role of the organization among themselves and afterwards with the relevant external stakeholders

- Timing issues around when to start certain activities within the organization

The coach's philosophy shaped the approach substantially. On the one hand, managers need opportunities to discuss important issues of work and life within the framework of confidentiality. On the other hand, she explains, individual coaching often focuses too much on the person rather than on their context – "the single manager is often trying to deal with challenges which in their true nature are really more organizational challenges. By focusing very much on the function – that is, the specific role of the manager and their unit as part of the organization – and by dealing with the main themes at the relevant management team level, the work also brings results in the form of organizational development."

It was agreed from the beginning that in this case there was no need for traditional team-building activities, which often lead to good experiences but do not necessarily create a learning environment for the team or connect to the daily work. This team's need was to work more effectively and efficiently together, to ensure organizational learning and new actions, and to focus on leadership related to the employees.

The goal set by the director and his management group was simply to professionalize themselves as individuals and as a team in relation to leadership, managerial and structural issues.

At the beginning of the programme most members of the management team felt confident that this was a good process. A few were a little nervous, but clear information and the process of creating common ground rules during a first round of individual meetings with the coach before the final commit-ment to the programme helped ensure a good start.

The work has now run for a year, all the managers have had the offer to continue with their individual coaching, and eight out of nine have chosen to do so for least half a year more. The coach can still bring up new themes, and now they have also made it a regular part of their meeting agenda to bring up what each of them sees as possible themes that should be dealt with.

The key lesson is that the model works! Creating synergy and bringing organizational development dimensions into the coaching by collecting and working on the main themes resulted in rapid organizational development and better cooperation among the managers. One specific insight was: "It's a relief to get rid of the feeling that all the challenges are mine and that it's up to me to find things out. With team coaching I have realized that many of the challenges are really organizational ones and we in the team have to work them out together!"

The only real difficulty in daily life for all of the team has been to hold on to the high priority of having their regular weekly meetings in a busy and unpredictable political world. Time for dialogue is essential, if you want common learning.

Finally, it should be stressed that this model of combined team and individual coaching probably only works and brings organizational development synergies if:

◆ the same coach is used during the whole process; and

◆ the coach is very skilled at keeping the ground rule around confidentiality.

This case study was written by Sonja Daugaard, an experienced consultant and executive coach, as well as a partner at Refflect, based in Denmark. Her email address is: sonja.daugaard@refflect.dk.

Relationship scope

It's obvious that team coaching involves more people, but there is an additional dynamic: coaching between team members. Team coaching works best when it stimulates and supports the coaching habit. One of the most useful devices I have found is to identify issues during one-to-one coaching that have significance for the team as a whole. I then encourage the individual to coach the rest of the team through the same evolution of thinking that he or she has experienced. This not only shares the learning, it also deepens and expands the learning that the individual extracts.

Reaching decisions

In many teams, a decision can be made with widely varying degrees of understanding and commitment. This phenomenon can be seen particularly starkly when the team is composed of multiple nationalities.

A DECISION OR A CHALLENGE?

A manager in a chemicals multinational described the situation thus: "We spent four hours arguing the pros and cons of different solutions relating to cross-border sales, then the European vice-president said we had to have a common policy for the region. He got everyone to say what their top two priorities were. He pulled those together into a logical policy representing the majority view on each point. Then he asked 'Do we have a decision?' Everyone said yes. Two months later, there was more chaos than before. The Germans and the Danes stuck to the policy rigidly, complaining at any apparent infringement by other countries; the English and Spanish kept looking for ways around the policy – keeping to the letter but not the spirit; and the French simply treated it as advisory and went on doing what they had been doing before, but a bit more circumspectly."

While allowing for the nationality stereotyping (the manager himself was Dutch, making for an even more volatile mix) the experience illustrates a universal truth – one person's decision is someone else's challenge!

Improving the quality of an individual's decision making is a relatively simply matter of developing insight (for example into how emotions influence decision making) and more rigorous processes of analysis and problem solving. At a team level, there is an additional dynamic. People operate at different speeds, both generally and on specific issues. Multiple inner dialogues need to be brought together into one open dialogue. The critical coaching question is the same as with individual coaching, but much more important. That question is: "Are you ready to make and commit to a decision now?" The regional vice-president in the example above made the fatal mistake of using his authority to force a decision when the team was not psychologically ready to commit to it.

This is also a major problem for an external team facilitator (see below), who tends to have a vested interest – reputation or because that is what they are being paid for – in ensuring that the team reaches clear decisions within the time period allotted. It may often be better to explore the conditions under which each team member would be willing to give full commitment to a solution, then create time for them to reflect and prepare for a subsequent dialogue based on those insights. The simple matrix in Figure 3.1 can be a useful way of getting this message across to the team.

FIGURE 3.1

DECISION QUALITY

	Low commitment & understanding	High commitment & understanding
Good decision	Benefits lost through poor implementation	Rapid and effective implementation
Poor decision	Confusion	Rapid implementation of the wrong thing

A large government department had already invested in one-to-one coaching for its leadership tier. Measurement data from the first phase of this programme had revealed a general deficiency in performance management. Team coaching was proposed because it was a cost-effective method of addressing this specific need, and because it offered an opportunity to learn by sharing experience.

Two prospective participants said they would prefer a session dedicated to them and their direct reports, rather than a mixed session. The organization was happy to agree to this. One of these two teams is the focus of this case study.

The team in question was a newly merged regional team. Its members came from all over the organization, including two brand new employees. The coaching session was aimed at helping team building and developing a shared philosophy for performance management. The team members knew they all had very different experiences on this subject. The coaching would enable them to find common ground and appreciate cultural differences. The external coach – Annette Gardner, from SKAI Associates, a leadership development consultancy – was already very conversant with the organization, so was able to help the team contextualize its discussions.

The team members debated whether their ultimate boss should be included or not; they decided against because they wanted the freedom to explore openly all the difficulties they were having. They were a very broad set of people and some were initially sceptical. They weren't used to anything like this, being more familiar with a command-and-control style rather than being coached to decide on their own solutions.

Given the seniority of the coachees, the assumption was made that "how to"-style training was irrelevant, and that any deficiencies in their performance management were not down to lack of knowledge about the subject. The approach was thus to focus on what was stopping them deploying that knowledge effectively.

The goals for the coaching sessions were set by the organization's human resources department and were:

◆ To create personal learning outcomes that were then delivered on

◆ To generate high levels of commitment to follow through

◆ To establish "buddying" arrangements to provide ongoing support for practice

◆ To ensure that participants felt very supported in their endeavours

◆ To cover certain specific topic areas

The initial coaching session was a full-day event. A follow-up session three months later took two hours. In the meantime, buddy pairs worked together to continue the learning process and to implement actions agreed during the initial coaching. In essence, this was co-coaching. At the mid point, participants shared their progress in a structured email exchange.

The team members found that they gained particular value from sharing each other's prior experiences, and from talking openly about real-life issues that they had in common. Given that they didn't know each other very well, finding the courage to share things that weren't being successful on their own patches was difficult (but worthwhile). Realizing that they could call on each other for help – that they were not the only ones with these problems – was an important step forward, and creating support agreements within the team reinforced this. Some members also revised their priorities on how important it was to tackle performance issues in their direct reports; as a result, they faced up to and sorted out major personnel problems that they had been avoiding.

In the follow-up session, instead of having a formal agenda the coach found that it was more effective to follow where the team's energies were. It was a useful lesson that sometimes pursuing even an agreed agenda may not be optimal, if something else is at the forefront of people's minds. The post-project evaluation also provided the lesson that telephone or e-coaching for individuals and buddy pairs would have been a useful additional resource.

Based on the experience of these team-coaching events, SKAI has distilled the distinctions between the two processes, outlined in Table 3.1.

TABLE 3.1

DIFFERENCES BETWEEN INDIVIDUAL AND TEAM COACHING

ASPECT	ONE-TO-ONE COACHING	TEAM COACHING
Preparation	A thorough "set-up" via HR always helps (what organization expects, logistics, closure, what coaching is/isn't, monitoring etc.). In practice it often doesn't happen, but a good coach's processes can compensate for this somewhat.	Preparation and set-up are more important. Setting the scene for the leader and the individuals in the team as to why the coaching is taking place is crucial, and has to be absorbed over time and related to a clear and obvious business need. Strong sponsorship from senior management helps here. Without this the team is often far from coachable and it can be impossible to get anywhere really meaningful.

TABLE 3.1 (CONT.)

ASPECT	ONE-TO-ONE COACHING	TEAM COACHING
Goal setting	A relative straight-forward part of the usual coaching process. Changes can easily be incorporated during coaching if needed.	It is necessary to identify where the team is and collectively where it wants to go. (Teams often ask for help on specific problems, rather than general development.) A narrower scope of issue for consideration needs to be established for a team – this helps many minds move from one stage to the next.
Leaders	The coach's boss should be involved, ideally via a three-way meeting at the start and at further intervals, as well as giving feedback and encouragement as changes are implemented.	The leader requires discrete coaching on how to interact with the team – up front and throughout. The coach must take care not to replace the leader.
Dynamics	The coach has limited opportunity to role-model behaviours and techniques (but can do some).	The coach has more opportunity to demonstrate desired team member behaviours. The psychology of decision making in teams (groupthink, conflict avoidance, cultural issues etc.) makes it harder for a team to recognize the need to change its collective outlook or approach.

TABLE 3.1 (CONT.)

ASPECT	ONE-TO-ONE COACHING	TEAM COACHING
Coach activities	Develop goals, define action plan required, develop necessary skills, support and challenge, give feedback, offer perspective, manage closure.	The same but much more requirement for facilitation skills – involving everyone, managing conflict, summarizing points of view far more often (different people listening at different times).
Coach abilities	Strong empathy and relationship skills are crucial, balanced with appropriate challenge. Highly tuned sensitivity and observational skills are useful.	The coach needs to be able to process a lot of information very fast and at a more macro level – observing dynamics among people and of the group, as well as those between coach and group. Overly highly tuned observational skills are not helpful – information overload results and the coach is ineffectual.

This case study was written by SKAI Associates, a leadership development consultancy that provides off-the-shelf and bespoke products for coaching, learning events and consulting. Contact info@skai.co.uk.

Models of team coaching

Virtually all the available research on team coaching in the work environment – and there is not a great deal – focuses on the role of the team leader coach or manager coach. Richard Hackman and Ruth Wageman[3] draw three key areas from this literature:

- The functions that team coaching serves for a team.
- The times in the task performance process when coaching interventions are most likely to have positive results.
- The conditions under which team coaching is most likely to facilitate performance.

In a previous study, Wageman and Hackman[4] looked at 288 teams in 88 organizations, asking teams and their leaders to rank how much attention the leader gave to four activities: structuring the team and its work, running external interference (i.e. protecting the team from external bother), coaching individuals and coaching the team. Coaching the team was the least common activity. The reasons, they suggest, are that leaders underestimate the benefits of team coaching and lack skills in performing the team coaching role.

Wageman and Hackman identify a range of approaches to team coaching, each having pluses and minuses. These fall on a spectrum of directiveness and non-directiveness (see Figure 3.2).

In the most directive, **operant conditioning** team coaching,[5] the coach gives instructions about how the team should behave, monitors its performance and gives praise, criticism or other forms of positive or negative reinforcement. This "tell" style of team coaching can be effective, but it is unlikely in most circumstances that the entire team will be at such a low level of developmental maturity that it needs to be coerced into new behaviours. It may also be harder to make behaviours stick when the focus of performance improvement shifts elsewhere than if the team members took a proactive part in the learning process.

FIGURE 3.2

FOUR MODELS OF TEAM COACHING

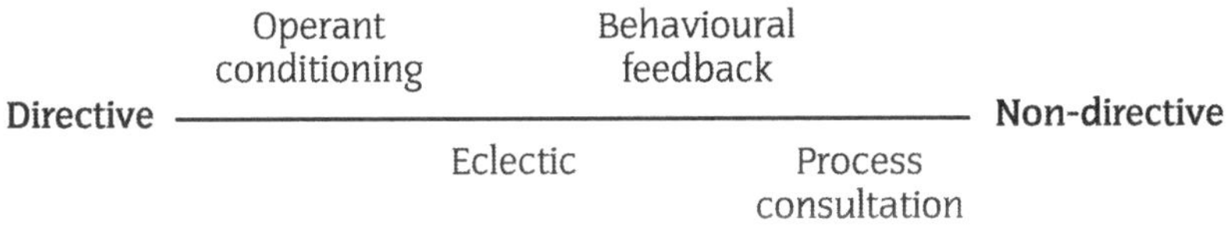

	Operant conditioning	Behavioural feedback	
Directive	————————————————————————————		Non-directive
	Eclectic	Process consultation	

Eclectic approaches codify the experience of practitioners and consultants into techniques that may help the team tackle specific issues of behaviour, roles or conflict, and lessen dependence on the team leader. These tend to be relatively directive, because the ownership of the process rests with the consultant.

A **behavioural feedback** approach, championed by Schwarz,[6] is a three-stage process consisting of observing the team at its task to identify behaviours that may impede performance; describing what the coach has observed and helping the team to discuss and draw conclusions from the feedback; and finally, leading a discussion about whether the team wants to change its behaviours and, if so, how it intends to both make and sustain the change. There is still an element of directiveness here, in that it is the coach, rather than the team members, who makes the observations, and hence the judgements about what is significant enough to note and what is not.

Process consultation, based on the work of Ed Schein,[7] helps team members analyse group processes on two levels simultaneously. On the substantive level, the analysis focuses on how behaviours and actions affect a specific problem; on the internal level, the focus is on the wider issue of understanding the implications of how members interact, for the functioning of the team as a whole. Here we enter into the heart of learning dialogue, with the team itself determining what is important, analysing the processes, and deciding what lessons to draw.

Additionally, the **developmental** approach to team coaching assumes that teams need help with different issues at different stages of their development and that teams are more open to interventions at some points in their developmental cycle than at others. Coaches adopting this philosophy pace their coaching according to the intensity of the work load. When people are at their busiest and most preoccupied, the coach spends time observing and gathering data to be used when they are more receptive.[8]

Wageman and Hackman define the functions that coaching provides for the team as:

"interventions that inhibit process losses and foster process gains in each of three performance processes: the effort people put in (motivation), the performance strategies (consultation), and the level of knowledge and skill (education)."

Notably absent in their analysis are any functions relating to interpersonal relationships within the team, on the basis, as discussed in Chapter 2, that such interventions "do not reliably improve team performance". When coaches focus attention on the quality of people relationships, Wageman and Hackman argue, they may improve attitudes and perhaps team spirit, but that does not necessarily have a significant, positive impact on the achievement of the team task.

Does this mean that coaches are wasting their time when they focus on relationships? The consensus of professional team coaches and their human resource clients in organizations with whom we have discussed the issues is that interventions at the relationship level are helpful – well beyond the extent one could dismiss on the grounds that "they would say that, wouldn't they?".

As is so often the case, these apparent contradictions between the results of empirical research and practitioner experience may well be the result of measuring different things. The key question, whether regarding an individual or a team, is: "What is the purpose of the behavioural intervention?" If the purpose is to improve the atmosphere and general sense of mutual goodwill within the team, the likelihood of the intervention having any significant impact on performance is probably small. The relationship between feeling good about colleagues and improving task performance processes is too vague to be useful. However, if the purpose is to address a specific, performance-related issue, in which there is a significant behavioural component to the process, a different dynamic is likely to apply. So behavioural coaching interventions that address issues such as coordination of activity, communication around specific tasks, or managing conflict that disrupts essential collaboration are likely to have a positive effect on performance. Relationship-focused coaching may also have a role to play in non-task-performance objectives, such as achieving compliance with corporate diversity goals. Even here, however, the impact of coaching is likely to be greater if it is focused on explicit skills (such as diversity dialogue) or processes.

Hackman and Wageman's summary conclusions about the conditions for effective team coaching are:

♦ There is room as well as opportunity to address key performance issues, such as motivation, strategy and acquiring knowledge and skills; that is, the restraints of the organization and task are not overburdening.
♦ The team is well designed, in a way that promotes rather than hinders teamwork.
♦ The focus of coaching is on issues and processes salient to the team tasks "and not on interpersonal processes or on processes that are not under the team's control".
♦ The timing of coaching interventions fits the cycle of team evolution.

Chapter 2 discussed various stages in how teams evolve. At certain points in their evolution teams are more open to coaching, because they are not overburdened with other calls on their attention and because issues conducive to coaching are current on their minds (see Table 3.2).

In the early stages of team formation, coaching is at its most effective when it focuses on clarifying the team task, gaining commitment, setting norms about how they will work together, delineating the team boundaries, roles and responsibilities, and building the initial motivation that underpins a good launch. Studies of airline crews[9] show that pre-flight briefings that engage all the team members in discussion and confirmation of roles help them perform better and coalesce more quickly than those that don't. While such briefings aren't the same as coaching, it is logical that the more intensive interaction of coaching would at least duplicate, if not improve on, this effect in all types of team.

THE MOST EFFECTIVE FOCUS OF COACHING OVER TIME

TIME	FOCUS OF INTERVENTION
Beginning	Motivational
Mid point	Consultative
End	Educational

By contrast, attempting to tackle strategy issues at this early stage seems doomed to failure. Teams that plunge right in to the task and reflect on their experiences later are more effective than those that strategize before they begin.[10] It seems that teams are not ready to address these big-picture issues until they have some experience under their belts.

At the mid point of the team's evolution, when the members have some experience of the task and have had time to develop anxieties about its direction and whether they will achieve the goal, the team is much more minded and prepared to discuss the strategic issues. Hackman and Wageman suggest that on-going teams, which have no mid point, also reach similar times in their cycle of work when they are more prepared to welcome coaching interventions targeted at reviewing progress, reassessing how they use their resources and talents, and fashioning new strategies. It seems that in some intuitive manner, akin to the way flocks of birds or schools of fish change direction in unison, the members of a well-functioning team come to an unspoken consensus that the time is ripe to create some collective reflective space. Quite how this happens is not clear, but we can speculate that one or two members start to feel the need to take stock and that this communicates itself in subtle ways to others. Interestingly, observation suggests that, while high pressure of work can delay this moment, this simply builds up the pressure.

The third transition point, at or near the end of the task or a sub-task, is when coaching needs to focus on helping team members codify, internalize and make use of the learning they have acquired doing the task. This is also a time for the coach to stimulate an accurate and fair assessment of the contributions that each member has made, and how they and the team have grown.

TEAM COACHING IN CONSTRUCTION

A recent action research project followed three teams in the construction industry as they underwent three sessions of team coaching. The short duration of the intervention made it difficult to identify any organizational benefits, but the teams reported greater self-awareness and better relationships with other teams as outcomes of team coaching. Although only 40 per cent of the objectives identified at the beginning of the intervention were achieved, two of the teams reported a much deeper level of thinking about issues relating to functionality and performance, resulting from the coach's challenging questions. One of the three teams found it much more difficult to cope with ambiguity and open dialogue. This team demanded far more structure and a more controlling style from their coach.

Factors that this project identified as important in the success of team coaching were:

◆ The team members took ownership of the process and responsibility for their own actions.

◆ They were committed to open-mindedness and independent thinking.

This research suggests, therefore, that as with individual coaching, success in team coaching depends on the skills and attitudes brought to the learning dialogue by both the coach and the team itself. Investigating the context of the team, to determine fears and other attitudinal or operational barriers to making the coaching process work, may be an important part of preparation.

Coaching or facilitation?

The role of team facilitator is often confused with that of coach. From time to time the coach may use facilitation skills, but it's important to differentiate the two roles, because they have different purposes and rely on a different type of relationship with the team. The variations are summarized in Table 3.3 overleaf.

The purpose of facilitation is to provide external dialogue management, to help the team reach complex or difficult decisions. The purpose of coaching is to empower the team to manage its own dialogue, in order to enhance its capability and performance. The facilitator is required – like a counsellor or therapist – to maintain a high level of detachment from the issue and to maintain their own focus and that of the team on process. In essence, they are catalysts. The coach, in contrast, helps the team or an individual create a separate space, where they can collaborate in seeking understanding of the issues. They are engaged with and may be changed by the ensuing dialogue and hence have a role more akin to a reagent. From time to time, the external coach in particular may need to adopt a facilitation approach and vice versa. However, clarity of role is likely to lead to greater effectiveness.

Team leading or team coaching?

It may seem strange to draw a distinction between team leadership and team coaching when such strong arguments are made for coaching being an integral part of the leader's role and routines. To make coaching a separate activity risks it becoming an optional add-on – which is exactly what happens in many teams now. However, there is a case for the team leader to recognize that they have to pay attention to both the day-to-day management of the team and the development of its collective capability and resourcefulness.

TABLE 3.3

TEAM COACH VERSUS TEAM FACILITATOR

ATTRIBUTE	TEAM COACH	TEAM FACILITATOR
Use/generation of feedback	Gives or helps team use feedback and also receives feedback	Helps team generate mutual feedback
Engagement	Within the team or engaged with the team	Detached from the team
Learning process	Shares the learning process	Directs/manages the learning process
Action/monitoring	Intellectual, emotional and practical support through the changes	Process support for the changes
Relationship	Reagent – coach acquires learning or change through the process	Catalyst – facilitator remains largely unchanged
Learning conversation	"Open" dialogue – structure generated from within	"Directed" dialogue – structure emerges from facilitator's observations
Enablers	Working within team dynamics	Understanding team dynamics
Outcomes	Team and individual achievement	Agreement on team direction and method

Table 3.4, which shows some of the main differences in approach between the leader-as-manager and the leader-as-coach, is broadly supported by other analyses of the two roles.[11]

TABLE 3.4

DIFFERENCES BETWEEN TEAM LEADING AND TEAM COACHING

ISSUE	LEADER-AS-MANAGER	LEADER-AS-COACH
Task goals	Sets goals for and with the team Develops commitment to the goals Reviews progress against the goals	Helps establish processes for setting and reviewing goals Explores alignment between personal, sub-group and team goals Helps explore the causes of setbacks/ progress failures
Learning goals	Establishes development needs of each team member Agrees personal development plans	Helps establish processes for integrating individual and team development plans
Visioning	Articulates the team's ambitions internally and to external stakeholders (e.g. higher management) Contextualizes the vision within the corporate vision	Tests the quality and viability of the vision and how it influences day-to-day activity Helps the team articulate the *values* behind its vision
Coordination	Ensures that everyone understands their roles and responsibilities Reviews and improves work processes, in consultation with the team Plans and strategizes	Gives feedback on processes and procedures, and on how the human factor affects these Helps the team question its processes and approaches Develops strategy skills
Problem solving and decision making	Demonstrates effective problem-solving and decision-making behaviours, by involving team members and achieving consensus	Helps the team improve its problem-solving and decision-making processes

TABLE 3.4 (CONT.)

ISSUE	LEADER-AS-MANAGER	LEADER-AS-COACH
Conflict management	Takes pre-emptive action to identify, discuss and prevent potential conflict Mediates and agrees rules that will reduce conflict	Gives feedback to ensure that conflict is recognized Improves the team's ability to manage conflict (and, where possible, use it beneficially)
Communication	Demonstrates effective communication Is available when needed Creates opportunities for communication to occur	Helps the team understand the theory and practice of communication Helps investigate and learn from communication failures
Learning processes	Ensures the team takes time to reflect and review	Helps the team build the skills and processes of reflective dialogue
Boundary management	Protects the team from external threats and interference Acquires resources	Helps the team review and improve its boundary management
Performance management	Clarifies expectations of performance Conducts appraisals Recognizes and rewards performance	Explores the influences on performance at both individual and team levels

BACK TO THE SPORTS COACHING ANALOGY

Nancy Katz, a Harvard academic who has studied sports and work teams in depth (see also Chapter 2), maintains that the effective team coach in both situations focuses on two critical tasks: how to motivate the team and how to structure its work.

The most successful sports teams have coaches who promote both cooperative behaviours and healthy competition. Unhealthy teams had a poor balance between these two elements.

Effective coaches also:

- **Orchestrate some early wins**. In two-thirds or more of sports fixtures studied, depending on the sport, the team that leads at half time goes on to win the game. Research by Hackman[12] shows that teams fall into "self-fuelling spirals" where early wins promote confidence and a winning streak and early failures promote a losing streak.

- **Break out of losing streaks**. Because downward spirals can kick in so easily, workplace leaders need the skill to restore confidence equally quickly and with confidence. Work by Lindsley, Brass and Thomas[13] reveals that failing teams define their problems as stable (i.e. based on a circumstance that is unlikely to change) and uncontrollable (beyond their ability to influence). Changing perception of problems and looking for the opportunities are the keys to reversing the downward spiral.

- **Carve out time for practice**. Katz promotes the concept of "intelligent failure" – learning by conducting lots of "small, thoughtfully planned experiments".

- **Call half time**. Periodic review, and especially review at the mid point of a project, provides a valuable opportunity for regrouping and pacing work.

- **Keep team membership stable**. Ralph Katz[14] found that group longevity significantly influenced team effectiveness.

- **Study the game video**. Effective coaches analyse what went right and wrong and how the team works together. A useful idea is to break the team into several sub-groups,

each of whom reviews performance, thus providing several different perspectives. Changing the composition of
the sub-group changes the perspective, providing continuous new learning.

The sporting analogy (with the provisos suggested in Chapter 2) gives us three options for where a coach is situated vis-à-vis the team. The most hands-on option is on the field, as an integral part of the team – "first among equals". The implications of this role include an emphasis on day-to-day activity and immediate skills, and a corresponding difficulty in taking a strategic or innovative perspective.

The second option is on the touchline, giving encouragement, observing the detail of play and providing feedback and advice at intervals. The coach in this scenario is able to step back from the play, observe both individual and group performance, and help the team reflect on tactics and on how each member interacts with their colleagues.

The third option is in the grandstand. Here, the coach is a bystander to the play, unable to influence it directly, but able subsequently to help the team adopt a multi-perspective, strategic approach and to link these understandings to wider themes of personal and group performance and development.

These three positions relate quite closely to the job roles of work team leader, team manager and external team coach. Each is a team coach, but with a different skills requirement based on three factors: engagement with the task, maintenance of perspective and nature of influence.

Team leader coaches are the most engaged with the task, so they need to have a good understanding of the processes and skills and to be technically competent in their own right. There is an expectation that they will have some expertise and that they will empathize with the struggles that newcomers to the team experience in adapting to the technical or operational requirements.

In terms of managing perspective, the team leader coach has to focus primarily on achieving the short-term and medium-term goals. But they also need to create opportunities where the team can be exposed to different perspectives – for example by spending time on customer visits – and to review the alignment between team and organizational goals.

Team leader coaches exert influence in real time. They are able to observe problems, errors and relationship conflict at first hand and to respond immediately. Hence they make stronger connections between action and effect. However, they have to be highly aware that they themselves may be a significant part of the team or individual performance problems; and that a certain amount of detachment is needed to recognize and address some behavioural dysfunctions within the team. Team leader coaches are also likely to exert a strong influence as role models, so they need to manage the role-modelling process in a proactive rather than passive manner.

Manager coaches engage with the task by providing direction, clarifying the link with organizational goals, aspirations and values, and providing both task-related and behavioural feedback. Their ownership of the task is at a different level from the team leader coach, more closely related to the outcomes of team efforts than the detail of the processes employed. Their need to manage upwards as well as below gives them a wider perspective, and their relative separation from the day-to-day action, along with their interaction with stakeholders outside the team, allows them to observe both process and behaviour more dispassionately. They influence primarily through suggestive and stimulative styles of coaching, motivating performance by expressing belief in the team's capabilities and raising horizons as to what it can achieve.

The **external team coach** operates at one more stage of removal from the task. They have very little need to understand the technical processes, except insofar as they shape the nature and degree of interdependence between team members. They bring a wider perspective that stimulates consideration of more radical options and allows for deeper investigation of cause and effect, both process and behavioural, and at the interface between. Like manager coaches, they operate through suggestive and stimulative coaching styles, but with special emphasis on the latter, with the aim of creating insight that impels the team and its members to action.

Team building or team coaching?

A great deal of money is spent on team building, although it is often unclear what is meant by the term. In theory at least, team building aims to create opportunities for team members to reaffirm individual and collective commitment, to build respect and esteem for their colleagues and to align more closely with common goals, with the result that the team performance improves.

The evidence for the efficacy of team building is mixed at best. It does seem to improve relationships between team members, but this does not necessarily translate into sustained productivity or performance gains. Part of the problem is a constant change of team membership: each newcomer creates a need to start the process again. Another factor may be that team building is often a relatively shallow activity, separated by long intervals of "work as normal". So while the deeper behavioural or interpersonal issues that create faultlines within the team are temporarily addressed, they gradually re-emerge and find expression in other ways. By contrast, frequent coaching dialogue is able gradually to address deeper issues and revisit them to prevent symptoms recurring. Team building and team coaching are compared in Table 3.5.

Outward bound types of team-building exercises appear to work because they tap into primordial instincts of cooperating to survive. Leaving aside gender issues (for example assumptions of appropriate group behaviour being based on a masculine perception and norms), where higher team cohesion results it relates to the generation of an "us against the world" spirit, which may not be beneficial in the wider workplace. Teams with such high emotional cohesion may, for example, be much more unrealistically positive than is normal about their own abilities compared to those of commercial competitors.

TABLE 3.5

TEAM COACHING AND TEAM BUILDING COMPARED

ATTRIBUTE	TEAM COACHING	TEAM BUILDING
Purpose	Effectiveness of task delivery and collaborative behaviour	Improving collaborative behaviour
Focus	Internal and external to the individual and team	Primarily internal
Learning process	Activities related to the work task	Activities unrelated to the work task
Reflective practice	How do we get things done together? How do we learn together?	How do we understand ourselves and each other? How do we get on together?
Role focus	Task roles and learning roles in the team	Task roles in the team
Learning conversation	"Open dialogue" – structure generated from within	"Directed dialogue" – structure emerges both from within and from a facilitator's observations
Typical time horizon	Over the period of a task or growth phase of the team – multiple small interventions	Fewer (often one), more intensive observations over a few days
Outcomes	Making practical use of applying appreciation and valuing of each other's contribution to work tasks	Appreciation and valuing of each other's contribution

Team coaching can negate the downsides of traditional approaches to team building by helping people understand and manage the social dynamics of the team, by introducing healthy doses of realism when appropriate, and by sustaining members' curiosity about the task, each other and the environment in which they work together.

THE WRONG WAY ROUND THE WORLD

The Global Challenge is known formally as the World's Toughest Yacht Race and runs every four years. It involves 12 identical yachts competing to sail west around the world – the most difficult route. Each yacht has a small number of experienced sailors and a crew of inexperienced volunteers, whose ages may range from early 20s to late 50s or beyond.

Will Carnegie, an experienced young sailor, was given the task of captaining *Veritas*, one of the yachts completing in the race in 2000. His crew of 18 included a 58-year-old man and a middle-aged former Pan's People dancer, Babs Powell, both of whom Carnegie turned to – although they knew next to nothing about sailing – as coaches on a range of issues relating to motivating the team and establishing the social cohesion and mutual commitment they would need to undertake the gruelling task ahead of them.

As part of his role in coaching the team itself, Carnegie brought its members together on land before they even set foot on the ship. His initial task was to achieve both a common sense of purpose and a common set of values. He was shocked to find that, to begin with, the team had neither.

His own goal was to win the race. That of the oldest crew member, Robert, was "to survive and conquer my biggest physical challenge". Tina, a 32-year-old marketing manager, wanted "to be on the winning yacht". Another crew member, Stephen, said, "I want my wife to have enjoyed every port of call" – it was important to him that his family were able to participate in his great adventure.

Says Carnegie: "It forced us to see the opportunities each of the others could bring to the task. We had to construct a culture in which diversity could be seen as a positive factor. We had to make the goal inclusive of everyone. Eventually, we agreed that: 'We aim to win the race in a safe and successful manner, capitalizing on our full team potential and to share our adventure with our wider family.'" Instead of being a flaccid compromise, the breadth of the combined goal gave each of the crew an expanded vision of what success meant for both them and their colleagues.

In the same way, a set of team values emerged: "recognition, punctuality, humour and excitement, discipline and safety, open and honest communication, second efforts" (i.e. going beyond the maximum effort to get things done). These were to stand the crew in good stead as it battled through hurricanes and other natural challenges – and especially when a freak wave injured two of the team, forcing the yacht to return to Sydney. Now last in the competition, the crew adopted a new goal – to complete the race without coming last – which they just achieved.

Carnegie's role as leader was to coach and be coached, using the diverse talents of the team to maximum advantage. Coaching in this environment involved constantly helping people evaluate the challenges they faced and their own responses to them against the goals and values that the team had set itself. Part of this, even in the most hectic periods of activity, meant finding space for reflective dialogue, both one to one and the whole crew together. For example, at one point, still lagging at the rear in the race, Carnegie stopped the ship for half a day to reevaluate, reassess the goals and reaffirm the values. The investment paid off in renewed vigour, enthusiasm and team cohesion.

Encouraging an environment where the team can coach the leader is easier said than done. Carnegie remembers feeling indignant when on an early training sail, a relatively inexperienced crew member suggested a different way of changing a sail. "Initially I felt like dismissing the idea – how could a 'rookie' understand the complexities of a sail change – after all, I had been sailing for 25 years!" It was an important lesson for Carnegie, who watched as the idea evolved through discussion into a process that was eventually adopted as standard procedure for the entire race. He says: "For me it was about encouraging openness and discussion. I made a point of sharing what I had learned from this lesson with the crew and was honest about the threat I'd felt. This in turn encouraged further openness and idea sharing.

"The openness that we tried to create was really important for confronting fear, a real issue on a race so challenging. In Buenos Aires I spent hours running one to ones with the crew before heading south to Cape Horn. I discussed fear with many of the crew. The next day one of the crew, Debbie, asked 'How are *you* feeling?' I was a little taken aback – this was the first time anyone had asked me, the leader, and was in many ways a question I had never had to answer. It was a great question to ask and I learned from Debbie that the team were keen to find out how I was feeling about the leg ahead! Again a case of openness breeding openness and a lovely example of how crew members like Debbie could coach and support me.

"One of the other big lessons for me was realizing that the crew did not develop as a 'mass' and one style of coaching was not fit for all. For example, as we raced home towards the UK on the penultimate leg, I learned that in relation to several tasks on board the yacht various crew members needed much more hands-on coaching from me than others. This meant that I had to think much more about the needs of individuals as well as the team. Too often I assumed that one size fitted all when actually everyone had different needs.

"The main benefits of a coaching style were the outcomes: one of the skippers in the previous race had joked that his goal for the last leg of the race was to spend the entire leg in his bunk! At sea I began to understand what he meant: initially the demands on me as a coach were huge in terms of time and effort and often distracted me from the tasks in hand. This investment, though, began to pay off as we raced around the globe and by the last leg I could spend far less time coaching and more on the strategic and tactical side of the race – or, if I chose, in my bunk! In summary, the investment up front bought me time later as the crew became less dependent on me for decisions and actions."

Coaching the top team

It's debatable whether the executives or the directors of an organization really constitute a team. Jon Katzenbach,[15] a US authority on the dynamics of senior teams, maintains that "all of the CEO's direct reports can seldom if ever constitute an ongoing real team". He writes:

"The CEO invariably functions as the single leader of a group whose membership is based on formal positions rather than on individual skills, whose purpose and goals are indistinguishable from the overall corporate purpose and goals, and whose behaviours are determined actively by individual accountability."

Whether they are a group or a team, however, the executives in particular need to work closely together to produce results for the organization. The coach to a top team needs to recognize the different dynamics of its decision-making and collaborative processes.

The coach also needs a set of additional skills and knowledge relating to corporate governance and strategic process. Here we get into the murky waters of how much a coach needs to understand and empathize with the environment, circumstances and demands on the client group and how much can be covered simply by using good coaching technique. The feedback from clients is consistently that a coach is only credible at this level if they have practical experience of sitting around the top table, or extensive experience observing top teams or boards at work. When dealing with individuals, the nature of the learning need may sometimes be focused on behavioural change, which can be tackled without reference to the business strategy or the marketplace. When dealing with the top team, however, strategy and strategic thinking are core to the issues under discussion, as is at least a basic awareness of the principles and practice of corporate governance.

Much of my own coaching of top teams has revolved around establishing and pursuing a board development plan, raising the board members' capability to deliver what the organization and its stakeholders need from them. The process is outlined in Figure 3.3.

The starting point – the initial coaching question – is: "What does this organization have to do really well to achieve its objectives now and in the future?" Based on this, the coaching conversation attempts to develop an understanding of what competences and capabilities the team expects to have and need in the future, and to compare these with what it has and needs now. Feedback from people in the next two layers is an important part of this conversation.

The gap at both points can be filled in several ways. The team can import new recruits (in which case it has to consider how it will find them and help them fit in), either from the external market or by bringing along internal talent. It can also provide individual development where appropriate, or it can address learning needs as a whole-team issue.

The outcome should be a detailed development plan for the top team as a whole, in which individual and collective learning are integrated. A final stage of the coaching conversation is to review the

FIGURE 3.3

A BOARD DEVELOPMENT PLAN

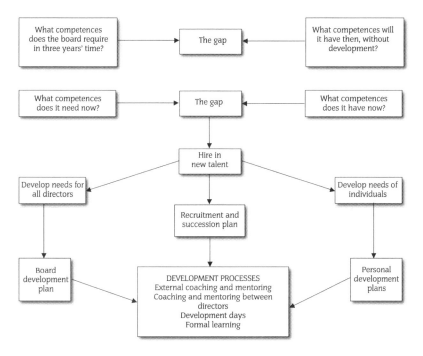

top team development plan against the business priorities identified at the beginning, and to consider how the top team wants to use this plan to stimulate more effective learning behaviours across the organization as a whole. The notion of being role models for learning is sometimes quite alien to senior managers, but it is one that most people eventually take on board.

COACHING THE BOARDS OF FAMILY BUSINESSES IN NORWAY

In 2003 Innovation Norway (www.invanor.no) in collaboration with a Norwegian bank, invited companies to take part in a pilot programme of board development, including coaching. Lilliann Andreassen,[16] an executive coach with an extensive background in corporate governance, took on the role of coach to three companies, of which two were family businesses. One family business was in a generation transition –

the father, who owned the business, had appointed his son as general manager and was in the process of handing over the reins. The other was run by a female entrepreneur. One is consistently profitable; the other operates in a market with frequent cycles of boom and bust.

The aim of the project was to help the board in each case to improve how it worked and to establish a strategic focus and stronger control over the business. The role of the coach was to help the board develop the self-insight to manage this change. Andreassen attended every board meeting for a year, intervening to ask questions that improved the quality of discussion between directors, and helping them review the processes, behaviours and outcomes of the meeting. At the very beginning of the project she also conducted a detailed study of each board, using a template of more than 50 key questions relating to the strategy, boardroom processes and so on, to understand its dynamics. She spent considerable time building trust and rapport with each of the board members and ensuring that they understood that her role was to coach, not to be a consultant or a non-executive director.

A large part of the coaching role was acting as devil's advocate and bringing issues to the table. Frequent questions included "What exactly are you avoiding here?" and "Do I have your permission to name what isn't being said?"

In one company, a significant issue was resistance from the leader of the board against professionalizing the finance function, even though the financial data presented to the board was inadequate for decision making. This person, who owned a small proportion of the shares, had a role conflict, because he was employed one day a week as finance director. In the other company, the owner/entrepreneur felt guilty about making money. Gentle coaching challenged this belief set and led her for the first time to set targets for return on investment.

In due course, it was recognized that both general managers needed individual coaching as well. The issue was discussed with and agreed by the board, without the coach present, and a set of protocols established to manage any potential conflict of interest or confidentiality. This one-to-one coaching provided an opportunity to be even more challenging, helping the general managers focus on how they would confront and deal with difficult issues in their teams and/or in their own approaches to the board and the business.

The outcomes for these two companies included significant improvements in board process and, in one case, a substantial turnaround in profit from zero to 17 per cent of turnover. Both were seeking non-executive directors at the end of the year, in part to replace the probing they had received from their coach.

For Andreassen personally, the outcomes included a great deal of learning, about small businesses and about how to manage group and individual coaching in the same team. A specific lesson was that, in the client's interests, it is not always possible to stay in coaching mode throughout a board meeting. From time to time, it is necessary to step out of the role and into advice giving. However, she learned that, when doing so, it was important to signal and ask permission for the change of role. She also made a point of gaining feedback from the board about the appropriateness and manner of these non-coaching interventions.

What effective team coaches do

Those few writers who have taken an analytical approach to the role of the external team coach in the working environment come to different conclusions. Perry Zeus and Suzanne Skiffington[17] present a model of the team coach as a combination of facilitator (of problem solving, conflict management and interpersonal relationships), monitor (of goals, obstacles and achievements) and coordinator (of team activities and of liaison with external management) – a relatively hands-on, relatively directive and didactic approach that begins and ends with reporting to a managerial client outside the team. Their recommended process consists of six steps, as follows:

1   Meeting the management client to establish the context of the team's operation and the organization's goals.
2   Meeting with each team member individually to identify issues from their perspectives.
3   First meeting with the team, to identify expectations, agree rules and procedures for team coaching and understand the coach's role.
4   Second coaching meeting to identify barriers to achieving the team goals.
5   Beginning the regular team coaching sessions, each one focusing on a specific issue (with the coach introducing new knowledge and behavioural skills).
6   Reporting back at intervals (at least twice) to the management client.

This approach contrasts radically with that taken by solutions-focused coaches, who see coaching not as something done *to* the team, but *with* the team. A solutions focus is closely allied to appreciative inquiry. It starts from four key assumptions:

◆   Focus on solutions, not on problems or causes of problems.
◆   Build on success – if something works, do more of it.
◆   Illuminating resources – identifying relevant skills that can be applied to the solution.
◆   Finding new perspectives – changing the focus of awareness to identify different options and possibilities.

The solutions-focused team coach helps the team extract from its experience the strengths and characteristics of its behaviours and processes when things are going well. They use questions such as:

◆ What positive moments were there in this gloomy period?
◆ What happened to make them different?
◆ What can we learn from these highlights that would help us tackle the issue differently?
◆ How could you create more of those moments? How could you make them the dominant theme?
◆ If you had already resolved the problem, what would you and others have done?

Solutions-focused coaches also use scales differently.[18] Whereas most coaches use a scale of 1 to 10 to get people to decide where they are and where they want to be, these coaches use a scale from 10 (the ideal state) to 1 (the exact opposite). They then ask questions such as:

◆ How did you get to the point of the scale where you are now?
◆ What did each of you contribute to getting to this point?
◆ What resources can you call on to ensure that you don't drop below that point?
◆ What resources could you call on to take just one step towards the ideal?
◆ How would you know you had achieved that step up the scale?
◆ What would your future selves advise you to do to maintain progress up the scale?
◆ What do you do now that doing more of would contribute?

Which approach works best? There isn't a simple answer: it depends on the organizational culture, the level of ability of the coach and the willingness of team members to break out of instinctive blame behaviours. It is probably true, however, that a really effective team coach will have the ability to work from both ends of this spectrum.

TABLE 3.6

KEY STEPS IN THE TEAM COACHING INTERVENTION

STEP	TEAM COACH'S ACTION	TEAM'S ACTION
Preparation	Establish what performance means in this context Establish how ready the team is for coaching	Consider willingness and readiness for coaching
Scoping	Clarify goals and timescales Establish how the outcomes of coaching will be measured Map the principal barriers and drivers to: • goal achievement • coaching effectiveness	Understand and commit to specific performance goals: task, learning and behaviour
Process skills development	Help the team acquire basic skills of learning dialogue	Commit to and practise skills of learning dialogue
Coaching conversations	Lead the coaching dialogue	Create reflective space: • calm time for coaching dialogue • calm time for subsequent reflection, individually and collectively
Process review	Briefly review coaching process at end of each session Review in more depth every third session	Consider and give open feedback about the coaching process Consider how they can make it more effective
Process transfer	Assist team to take more leadership of coaching conversation	Take more leadership of coaching conversation Increase emphasis on peer coaching and team self-coaching

TABLE 3.6 (CONT.)

STEP	TEAM COACH'S ACTION	TEAM'S ACTION
Outcomes review	Assist team to evaluate what has been achieved through coaching Give feedback on team's presentation to more senior management	Take responsibility for the outcomes of coaching and reporting them back to more senior management

A truly generic template for team coaching should incorporate what both the coach and the team need to do for an effective intervention. Table 3.6 is a bare-bones template that attempts to capture the key steps and incorporates some elements from both the hands-on and solutions-focused approaches, while remaining true to the spirit of coaching as a means of helping people do things for themselves. The first three elements – preparation, scoping and process skills development – do not have to be precisely sequential; it is more usual for them to be somewhat intermingled.

Most of the themes in this template are covered in more detail in the remaining chapters. However, it is practical to consider the first step – preparation – here, as an introduction to these chapters.

Preparing the team to be coached

As we discussed briefly in Chapter 1, it makes a positive difference to the effectiveness of both individual and team coaching if coachees have appropriate skills to help the coach help them. It is therefore useful in the early stages of team coaching to undertake an audit of the team's individual and collective skills in being coached and in managing learning dialogue. In general, the more previous exposure team members have had to effective coaching, in any form, the more responsive the team is likely to be to the idea of a team coaching intervention.

Some of the critical questions to test readiness for team coaching are outlined below.

TEAM READINESS FOR COACHING

- ◆ Does the team see itself as a team?

- ◆ If not, does it see value in becoming a team?

- ◆ Are members prepared to commit to tackling issues through open dialogue?

- ◆ Are there existing conflicts that need to be addressed before tackling the current problem?

- ◆ Is there a genuine desire for change?

- ◆ To what extent does the team understand the coaching process?

Becoming truly effective

Team coaching in the workplace is an exciting area in which to experiment and learn. It's important for the coach to recognize the differences between working with individuals and working with teams and to develop a portfolio of personal skills and approaches appropriate to this more complex coaching environment.

FINAL COACHING QUESTION

What learning would you need to acquire to become a really effective team coach?

CHAPTER FOUR

Coaching the learning team

"The ability to learn faster than your competitors may be the only sustainable competitive advantage" | **Arie de Geus, Shell**

"Learning should be in the service of action, not simply discovery or insight." | **Chris Argyris**[1]

Team learning is a key component of organizational learning. It simply isn't possible for the organization as a whole to learn if the teams within it aren't developing new knowledge and skills, and sharing these new resources with each other. I quoted Peter Senge in the Introduction, decrying the emphasis on individual learning in most organizations, and maintaining that the team is the crucial unit at which organizational learning takes place. Harvard University researcher Amy Edmondson,[2] of whom more later, describes organizational learning as a process of cascading team learning opportunities, independently carried out but interdependent in their impact on company performance.

Of course, teams are continuously learning from both their internal and external environments. However, there is a big difference between unconscious, unfocused learning and learning that is conscious, purposeful and directly related to the accomplishment of the team task. When members of a team all engage in purposeful learning-related behaviours, the team improves its ability to adapt to its environment and to operate effectively in that environment.

In the same way that people bring individual goals to the team and subsume these into shared team goals, they may have a range of learning goals that more or less align to team learning goals. For example, an employee in his late 30s was quite open about the reason he was in his current team:

> "I have spent time in IT, in buying and in sales. I now want to gain experience in account management, so that I have a rounded experience of the sharp end of the retail business. Then I want to transfer into training, where I will have increased credibility, because I've learned the hard way how the business works."

At one level, his learning goal was very different from those of his colleagues or the team as a whole. Yet recognizing this difference meant that his line manager could harness the employee's enthusiasm to learn quickly and widely. In addition, the employee was motivated to share his knowledge of other functions and the team was able to gain leverage towards fulfilling its goals through the relationships that he forged with the training function.

Team learning, then, is a process that can be managed for the benefit of individuals, the team and the organization. The circumstances under which alignment of goals occurs and the processes that the team and its coach can apply to maximize the quality and quantity of useful learning are the theme of this chapter. Or, as Amy Edmondson puts it:

> "Organizational learning can be seen as a process of cascading team learning opportunities, independently carried out but interdependent in their impact on company performance."

In much the same way that learning in general does not necessarily contribute to performance, team effectiveness isn't automatically an outcome of team learning. A lot depends on what the team learns, how it does so, and whether and how it applies useful learning. Table 4.1 separates out some of the differences in emphasis between

TABLE 4.1

DIFFERENCES IN EMPHASIS BETWEEN TEAM EFFECTIVENESS AND TEAM LEARNING

ISSUES IN TEAM EFFECTIVENESS	ISSUES IN TEAM LEARNING
Decision quality	Quality of reflection and dialogue
Innovation	Absence of power difference
Psychological safety	Psychological safety
Communication about task	Communication beyond the task
Using skills and knowledge	Creating and sharing skills/knowledge
Mutual support	Mutual learning
Managing interfaces outside the team	Importing external learning
Using diversity (e.g. to assign tasks)	Learning from diversity

team learning and team effectiveness. All of these issues are relevant to the team coach's role; all represent linkages that need to be made in helping the team become more competent. For example, decision quality is heavily reliant on the quality of reflection, innovation on the absence of power distance.

What is a learning team?

The concept of team learning is sufficiently immature that there are few considered definitions. Our preferred definition is "a group of people with a common purpose who take active responsibility for developing each other and themselves". A learning team is therefore not necessarily a work team; certain types of team, such as action learning sets or quality circles, may exist primarily for the purpose of mutual learning. In the workplace, most learning teams will, however, be work teams that recognize the importance of learning goals and processes to achieving task goals.

The key principles of learning teams drawn from our research are described below.

Learning goals, processes and outcomes have an owner

Although some learning occurs all the time, purposeful, functional learning requires ownership both by the team and by individuals within it. In our study of team learning behaviours, we identified a distinct cycle of activities, which effective learning teams engaged in and which were common to all six team types. We also identified a number of roles that members of the team played to support the learning process.

A wide variety of learning resources is used

People in learning teams are open to learning opportunities wherever and whenever they arise. They recognize the difference between learning and being taught. Learning opportunities arise from making mistakes, from asking naïve questions, from pursuing natural curiosity, from job shadowing, benchmarking visits and many other activities. People in learning teams tend to have a better balance between the four ways of learning illustrated in Figure 4.1.

A useful exercise in helping people appreciate the learning potential around them is to ask the team to list all the learning opportunities they can identify. Most teams (with a little encouragement) find at least 50.

The coaching questions that arise from this exercise include:

◆ How would we and our work benefit from making better use of more of these learning resources?
◆ What can and should we be doing to enlarge our repertoire of learning resources?

FIGURE 4.1

LEARNING METHODS

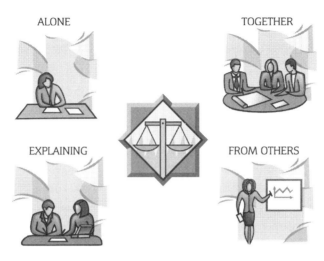

ALONE   TOGETHER

EXPLAINING   FROM OTHERS

images © 2007 Jupiterimages.com

People share their knowledge and learning

Members of learning teams are both positive about giving information to colleagues and proactive in offering help when it may be useful. There is a constant exchange of learning on both work and
non-work issues – learning is seen as a boundary-less responsibility.
People don't parade their knowledge, either, but they do ensure that
it is always available.

The leader creates an environment suitable for learning

Much of the writing about team leadership suggests that the "new"
leader is the team coach. To an extent that is true; but in practice,
the leader is *a* coach.

The distinction is important. The assumption that coaching is
done primarily by the team leader is highly disempowering. It also
doesn't reflect reality: most coaching is actually done by peers. The

FIGURE 4.2

COACHING RESPONSIBILITIES WITHIN THE TEAM

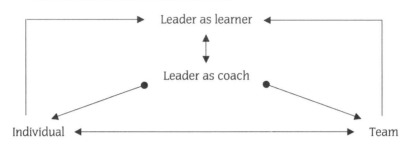

critical responsibilities of the team leader are to be an effective, positive role model for coaching behaviours; and to stimulate a climate where coaching is integral to the way the team carries out its daily tasks. One of the most powerful ways the team leader can establish this style is to be very open about their own learning needs and invite team members to provide reciprocal coaching (see Figure 4.2).

Dialogue produces more than discussion or debate

Most teams have some debate, a lot of discussion and very little real dialogue. The distinction between these three forms of conversation is elaborated below.

DEBATE, DISCUSSION AND DIALOGUE

Debate = having a fixed point of view and trying to convince others that it is right. Debate usually results in entrenching existing views and resistance to change.

Discussion = having an outcome you wish to achieve, but being willing to listen to and accept the validity of the other person's view. Discussion usually leads to modest changes in perception and to compromise.

> **Dialogue** = approaching an issue with as open a mind as possible, with a view to understanding other people's perspectives and perhaps creating a new perspective. Dialogue typically leads to commitment and willingness to change.

Reprinted with permission from Clutterbuck, D and Hirst, S (2003) *Talking Business*, Butterworth Heinemann, Oxford

Creating the habit of dialogue, as so elegantly championed by Chris Argyris,[3] Peter Senge[4] and others, takes time and courage. The skills of dialogue don't always come naturally: people need to learn them and practise them, and it's easy to relapse unless the whole team is committed to the process. Some of the ground rules of dialogue include:

◆ Reflective preparation
◆ Suspended judgement
◆ Mutual exploration
◆ Dancing at the edge of chaos
◆ Being simplex not simplistic

Reflective preparation is both physical and mental. It's very difficult to have an insightful conversation under excessive stress or when the body is in action mode. So it's important to remove the time pressures as much as possible and allow people to unwind. If dialogue is what you want, then paradoxically, having a detailed agenda may be highly counterproductive. A small, flexible agenda will almost always deliver more value in less time. (This is one of the reasons so many board meetings fail to address important issues in the depth needed: there are simply too many urgent but less important items on the agenda!) I sometimes ask teams to undertake brief relaxation exercises before beginning a dialogue.

The mental side of reflective preparation is about focusing on clear and meaningful outcomes, and on collaborative processes. Before the dialogue begins, everyone should have considered and be able to describe to the others in the conversation what they want to hear, to say, to achieve and to learn. They may also consider questions such as:

◆   What are my motivations in this conversation?
◆   Will those help or hinder the process of dialogue?
◆   What motivations do I fear others have, which might hinder the process of dialogue?
◆   What responsibility do I feel towards the rest of the team for ensuring a positive outcome from this conversation?

Suspending judgement is a critical skill of reflective listening. Making judgements is the end of an interaction, so people who make judgemental statements have effectively decided that the dialogue (if it ever was truly dialogue) is over.

Beliefs, attitudes and behaviours do not arise for no reason. They are the result of an intertwining trail of rational calculations and emotional experiences. Trying to understand this trail helps us appreciate the origins and logic of other perspectives – and hence to value both the perspective and the person in whom it is invested. An important element in suspending judgement is the recognition that no one is ever right: the truth changes with the perspective from which it is viewed. In much the same way, scientists recognize – or should do so – that today's explanation for physical phenomena is almost always only an approximation, which will be superseded by greater understanding and better theories in time.

The process of creating this level of understanding is one of **mutual exploration**: working collaboratively to map the geography of an issue from various perspectives, each of which serves to build insight into its nature. Sometimes this exploration takes people to places where they feel uncomfortable, or where there are simply too many ideas or perspectives to cope with easily. Persevering in this state – **dancing at the edge of chaos** – leads gradually to an understanding of patterns and linkages, in much the same way as a "magic eye" picture resolves itself from a jumble of shapes into a clear image.

At this point it is sometimes easy to relapse into simplistic assessments of the situation (e.g. "they don't care") and devalue the whole process. To maintain the impetus of dialogue, each participant seeks a **simplex** understanding, one that recognizes the complexity of the issue but identifies the basic structures in much the same way that the seeming chaos of the magic eye is made up of simple fractal shapes. This insight is the basis of a new, shared understanding of reality in relation to the issue – an acceptance and embracing of different viewpoints as important contributions to new and better ideas and solutions.

Described in this way, the process of dialogue can seem intensely difficult. But most people can and do learn to follow each of the stages and to build their ability to manage them individually and collectively.

Reflective space is allowed for

Reflective space is the time when dialogue – either internal to the individual or internal to the team – takes place. It is rare in the workplace to find reflective space occurring naturally. Thinking deeply is hard work, especially when it means challenging assumptions and beliefs, so it's not surprising that we find all sorts of convenient excuses to avoid it. Learning teams encourage time for thinking and questioning, both individually and collectively; moreover, they protect and cherish reflective space.

Reflection is very different from the typical group discussion that happens in most team environments. It is more considered, deeper and thinks about issues from a much wider range of perspectives. Normal team discussions often tend to be dominated by the need to get on with other, more immediate tasks; by process failures, such as ignoring externally available information or devaluing the knowledge or views of some team members; by deference to authority; and by failure to see the full picture.

Energy is spent on balancing the focus on task completion, learning and behaviour

Gravity is defined in physics as a very weak force, yet you don't have to fall very far for it to hurt, or to do yourself severe damage. When we ask managers and their teams to describe the forces acting on them, we typically hear that there is one strong force – getting the task done – and two weak forces – maintaining the pace of learning and managing behaviours. It's very easy to overlook the medium-term impact of failure to address these weaker forces, but they will inexorably reduce the team's ability to deliver the task, if they are not addressed. Unfortunately, the effect is often masked by frequent changes of targets. If the goalposts move often enough, it is easy not to notice that the game has changed.

Effective teams, as we saw in Chapter 2, recognize that over-attention to task and under-attention to learning have severe medium- and long-term dysfunctional effects.

Managers in our study of learning in teams described the conflict between task focus and focus on learning and behaviour as one of the most difficult they and the team have to manage. This classic urgent/important dilemma is made worse when teams are "lean" (which means frequently that the volume of work demanded exceeds the capacity of the team to perform it). Managers don't get rewarded for missing targets!

The descriptions by members of effective learning teams indicated a complex and constant interaction between these three forces (see Figure 4.3). Cooperative, supportive behaviours enhanced the team's ability to achieve the task goals; they also made it easier to learn from and with each other. Focus on the task goals stimulated clearer understanding of learning needs and task-appropriate behaviours. Focus on learning goals equipped the team and its members with skills and insight to be more task efficient and to re-examine strategy and tactics at appropriate times; they also equipped members with the behavioural skills to work together more effectively. In short, task, learning and behaviour were inseparable.

FIGURE 4.3

FOUNDATIONS OF THE HIGH-PERFORMING TEAM

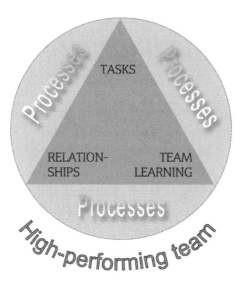

Over-emphasizing one focus at the expense of the others is not conducive to team performance, however. A team where everyone puts massive energy into being nice to each other is unlikely to face up to the issues that it most needs to address. A team that is overly focused on the task, as we have seen, is equally problematic. And, it seems, too much of a learning focus is not a good thing either.

Evidence from a study by Bunderson and Sutcliffe[5] suggests that over-emphasis on learning can compromise performance in the short term. The authors conclude that a strong learning goal orientation will lead to more task-focused, adaptive, mastery-oriented behaviours, whereas a performance goal orientation will lead to more ego-focused, instrumental and defensive behaviours. They summarize their findings like this:

"A group's... learning goal orientation is a robust predictor of learning related goals and behaviours pursued by team members... Teams with a stronger learning orientation will... tend to pursue a greater number of new ideas related to a wider range of team activities as well as ideas that represent larger digressions from current thinking and practice... Groups with an overemphasis on learning find that they suffer the costs of experimentation without gaining many of its benefits."

Members of teams in our study where continuous, substantial learning did take place talked about proactive behaviours to carve out space for reflection and socialization. In these teams, the manager and the team members ring-fenced "smart time" (opportunities to discuss and review activities with a view to working smarter, rather than harder) and "together time" (opportunities to build working relationships, to understand each other's capabilities and limitations, and to reaffirm supportive behaviours). They were convinced that this supported task achievement by:

◆ Clarifying the task and the priorities within it
◆ Preventing energy-sapping conflict
◆ Improving the quality of performance
◆ Maintaining a better balance between effectiveness and efficiency

We have not yet carried out empirical studies to test the accuracy of these perceptions, but logic and anecdotal evidence suggest that they are at least substantially correct. Team leaders and team coaches can help the team build resilience to excessive task focus by:

◆ Scheduling reflective space and social space into the team routines and making the case for them both within the team and to influential external stakeholders, such as more senior management. (Social space can be something as simple as providing a sandwich lunch once a week, so that people can meet and talk without a task objective, or to share work experiences informally.)
◆ Gathering evidence for the benefit of learning dialogue, in terms of improving task delivery.

- Engaging the team as a whole in determining how to free up the time of individual members to attend external learning events, such as courses, for the benefit of the team as a whole.
- Being role models for stepping back from their own tasks at appropriate intervals.

Alternative views of team learning

Other writers, coming from a different perspective, define team learning differently. For example, one describes it as:

> "an iterative team process in which information is 1) acquired, 2) distributed, 3) both convergently and divergently interpreted, and 4) stored and retrieved leading to a change in the range of the team's potential behaviors."[6]

In this definition, information acquisition is undertaken through passive scanning of the environment, to identify problems and opportunities; and through "probing", active enquiry. Distribution is the process of sharing information with other team members. Interpretation may be convergent (discussion leading to collective understanding and conclusions) or divergent (opening up new ideas and agendas). Storage and retrieval cover a range of processes that create "team memory".

The extent to which each of these activities contributes to learning within the team is unclear, but at least one study[7] indicates that storage and retrieval of learning is the most difficult process step and the one that most explains variations in team performance. The ability to manage this process step is related to the time people need to develop appropriate habits and establish a critical mass of common learning.

D'Andrea-O'Brien and Buono[8] conclude that

> "Team learning is the ability of members to share and build on their individual knowledge so that their collective

knowledge enables them continually to improve team performance as well as to discover, develop and implement completely new ways of doing business. Within this context 'unlearning' (i.e. discarding obsolete and misleading knowledge) can be just as important as learning new knowledge."

They point out that, while many managers talk about leading a team, it is more common for them actually to manage their direct reports as a group of individuals. The key characteristics of learning teams, these authors maintain, are that:

- They require an environment in which individual members are encouraged to experiment, learn from each other and develop their full potential.
- They extend this learning to include key stakeholders, such as customers and suppliers.
- They have a significant human resource component (i.e. they spend time nurturing and supporting).
- They continually undergo a process of development and transformation.

Other studies, which we will now explore, focus on the influence of team environment or climate, both internal and external, on team learning; and on the processes that support effective learning within the team.

Team learning and team knowledge

One of the roles of team learning is to expand and enhance the team's capability by increasing the breadth and depth of team knowledge: the collective information, expertise and experience of the members. It seems that teams have two types of team knowledge.[9] One is more permanent and stable, relating to the rules, concepts and so on to do with the task, the steps that need to be taken and when, and the strategy being pursued. It is generally acquired through common experience and leads to common expectations. The other is more situational – the almost intuitive interpretation of each other's cues and intentions as team members deal with a specific issue. It takes time to develop both of these forms of knowledge base, so short-duration teams, such as project teams, or teams where people don't normally work in close proximity to each other (development alliances or virtual teams) may struggle to develop it.

Another way of analysing team knowledge is as a mixture of **professional expertise** held by a specialist – perhaps the consultant in a clinical environment – and **collective knowledge**, which is much more distributed within the team. The problems with professional expertise include difficulties of miscommunication, unwillingness of team members to question decisions in someone else's area of expertise, and the scale of expertise loss when a team member leaves or is absent. Teams that over-emphasize professional expectation are therefore much more vulnerable over the long term with regard to performance than are teams built around collective knowledge. Table 4.2 overleaf shows some of the descriptive differences between these two approaches.

A common role for the team coach is to help a team move from the professional expertise model to a collective knowledge model, or to one that incorporates the best features of both models.

Some useful coaching questions around team knowledge include:

◆ What knowledge does this team need?
◆ How much of it do we have in explicit form and how much is held tacitly?
◆ Where do we have knowledge gaps?
◆ What is our process for translating tacit knowledge to explicit? How important is it to do so?
◆ What is our process for translating individual knowledge into collective knowledge?

- What individual or collective knowledge do we have but not exploit?
- Could we achieve the team task better if we did exploit that knowledge?

TABLE 4.2

PROFESSIONAL EXPERTISE AND COLLECTIVE APPROACHES TO TEAM KNOWLEDGE

KNOWLEDGE-EMBEDDING MODEL WITHIN THE TEAM KNOWLEDGE CONSIDERATION	PROFESSIONAL EXPERTISE MODEL	COLLECTIVE MODEL
Form of knowledge	Abstract, theoretical, education/training, standardized, context free, explicit, generic, highly rationalized and internally coherent	Hands-on experience, on-the-job training, less formal/theoretical, more limited causal understanding, context bound, distributed
Structure	Specialization, differentiation, deep (less broad), less overlap, individual	Considerable overlap, flexible and fluid utilization, highly diffused
Coordination and transmission	Multidisciplinary aggregation, owned knowledge, difficult to secure common experience and shared codes	Collective decision making, coordination achieved through mutual adaptation, knowledge generated and stored organically in team relationship

Reproduced with the permission of Professor John Sparrow, Knowledge Management Centre.

The climate for team learning

Our study of learning in work teams revealed a catalogue of reasons why learning didn't happen. The most common was that the pressures of the task – getting urgent jobs done – left no time for reflection or review. Other common barriers to learning included:

- Taboos: topics the team members had learned it was best to avoid
- A sense among team members that it was useless trying to change things
- Inadequate communication (e.g. routines that emphasized transactional communication in a virtual team, without corresponding relationship-building communication)
- Resource constraints (e.g. no access to learning materials or courses)
- Lack of skills in learning and in helping others to learn
- Knowledge hoarding: organizations that operated on a "need to know" basis
- A lack of "psychological safety": people being afraid to speak up, experiment or engage in constructive challenge
- Insufficient variety in perspective, or an unwillingness to listen to people with different perspectives

There is a significant challenge for the coach to help people overcome their instincts in order to both develop a rational evaluation of the learning potential of people substantially different from themselves, and to learn how to take advantage of the learning opportunity. Here we will discuss the last two barriers in particular.

Psychological safety and team learning

Psychological safety is "a shared belief held by members of a team that the team is safe for interpersonal risk taking".[10] One of the global experts on this topic is Amy Edmondson (see earlier in this chapter), who explains:

> "Team psychological safety involves but goes beyond interpersonal trust; it describes a team climate characterized by interpersonal trust and mutual respect in which people are comfortable being themselves."

Her studies of over 50 work teams show that the more people feel they can be open with their colleagues about work and interpersonal issues, the greater the learning that takes place and, as a result, the more effective the team is.

In teams with low psychological safety, speaking one's mind carries heavy risks. Admitting a lack of knowledge or asking for help may be seen as likely to result in a loss of prestige, being seen as incompetent, or being blamed for team failures. Raising issues that might cause a colleague to lose face is also a risk.[11] The potential cost of openness, in terms of threat and/or embarrassment, is greater than the reward for doing so, even when people know that the team and the organization will ultimately benefit from openness. A great deal of effort and numerous learning opportunities are lost because people are preoccupied with maintaining the social image that they feel is demanded by the group.

In teams with high psychological safety, by contrast, there is a willingness to address difficult issues, to manage conflict honestly and openly as a means of improving efficacy, to experiment and to both accept and learn from mistakes and failures. Edmondson describes "a team climate characterized by interpersonal trust and mutual respect, in which people are comfortable being themselves". It's no good if one or two people share this attitude set: to have any significant impact on team learning and team performance, the team as a whole must endorse and practise open behaviours and dialogue. These "shared group beliefs" provide the safety net for learning.

One of Edmondson's key conclusions is that coaching by the team leader is associated with team learning and psychological safety. Others are that team learning is associated with a "shared belief that one will not be blamed by other team members, who can be counted on to help each other and who are not punitive"; and that "a team's interpretation of others' intentions plays an important role in its openness to feedback; by believing others' intentions to be helpful rather than critical, the team is more likely to interpret negative feedback as friendly rather than unfriendly data."

Learning and diversity: Difference of perspective

It seems obvious that there are more opportunities for learning where people are different, but like most issues relating to teams, it isn't as simple as that. At an individual level, practical experience in coaching and mentoring tells us that the quality of relationships and the potential for learning are dependent on two factors: identity (personality, gender, racial and cultural background etc.) and experience (track record, knowledge, qualifications, interests etc.). This is illustrated in Figure 4.4 overleaf.

The problem is that too much similarity creates narrow opportunities for learning, even though there may be a high willingness on the part of both parties to engage in co-learning activity; and that relationships with high learning potential may have a lack of rapport between the individuals that prevents them valuing the other party as a learning resource.

Our negative reactions to diversity stem from a number of basic and powerful psychological drives. Our need to feel part of a group leads us to attribute negative qualities to those whom we perceive as different from ourselves – for example to under-estimate their intelligence, goodwill, honesty and competence – and more positive qualities to people whom we see as similar to ourselves. It's almost

FIGURE 4.4

RAPPORT VERSUS LEARNING

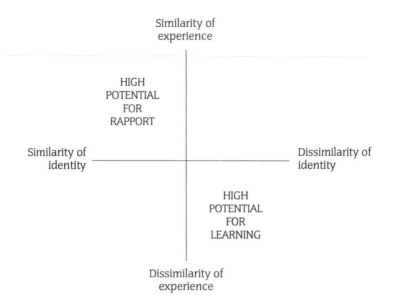

as if by criticizing people "like us" we are attacking our own self-image and self-esteem. Managers consistently over-estimate the capability and motivation of their own team compared to that of their competitors, and in so doing they become resistant to opportunities to learn from elsewhere. (This is more than "not invented here" – it is more "not worthy of learning from".) In short, we have an in-built, instinctive barrier to learning from difference.

These same phenomena apply equally within the team. Erica Foldy[12] draws on investigations of "diversity perspectives" in groups by Ely and Thomas[13] to review what enables learning in culturally diverse groups.

Group learning theory has been dominated in recent decades by Argyris and Schon's[14] concept of single-loop and double-loop learning, also described as Model 1 and Model 2 types of learning. The behaviours and frames of thinking in Model 2 learning – in effect, a means of bringing mental models to the surface for deeper understanding of learning processes – require reflection and open enquiry; in short, learning dialogue.

Factors that might impede culturally diverse groups from achieving Model 2 behaviours and attitudes, says Foldy, include the following:

- People feel more comfortable in groups where they are surrounded by people they perceive as more like themselves. When the group includes people who are not like them, trust is reduced. As a result, they are less likely to offer these others the benefit of the doubt, there is greater potential for conflict and open dialogue is difficult.
- Members of culturally diverse groups are more likely than others to differ in "how they define a problem, structure a discussion, view potential solutions, or come to a decision. These differences of opinion represent either a mother lode of creativity or a quagmire of conflict, depending on how the group handles conflict and differences."
- Members of the minority group may feel more aware of their identity and hence less comfortable or welcome.
- Members from the dominant culture may "consciously or unconsciously act in ways that reinforce their dominance in their conversational styles, decision-making processes, social interaction and so on".

Ely and Thomas define a diversity perspective as including

> "the rationale that guides people's efforts to create and respond to cultural diversity in a work group; normative beliefs about the value of cultural identity at work; expectations about the kind of impact, if any, cultural differences should have on the group and its work; and beliefs about what constitutes progress toward the ideal multicultural work group."

The three perspectives they identified are:

- **Discrimination and fairness** – where the organization or group focuses on recruitment or retention to redress past imbalances, but does not see value for work practices in surfacing and engaging with issues of difference.
- **Access and legitimacy** – "celebrating cultural differences, but in simplistic and narrow ways". For example, the company may employ Asian salespeople to sell to Asian customers.
- **Integration and learning** – this perspective sees difference as a source of growth, learning and insight for both individuals and the organization. The different experiences and viewpoints of employees are a resource for "rethinking primary tasks and redefining markets, products, strategies, missions, business practices and even cultures".

Foldy argues strongly for combining a high learning (Model 2) framework and an integration and learning perspective within work teams and for using these combined approaches to stimulate discussion about diversity. She proposes that learning takes place both *from* difference (how different approaches can change the way members think about their work tasks) and *across* difference, facilitating "learning about a host of things that may be unrelated to cultural differences".

Although Foldy has focused her review on racial difference, it is likely that the same general arguments could be made in relation to groups that are diverse by virtue of personality, discipline, education, sexual orientation or gender. Other recent studies[15] have established that highly diverse international teams can perform as well as highly homogeneous teams over the long term if they engage in Model 2 learning behaviours, which lead to the gradual evolution of a team identity that embraces differences.

When the source of diversity is based primarily on experience or expertise, rather than identity, a different picture emerges. Studies of collective team identification (defined as "the emotional significance that members of a given social group attach to their membership of that group"[16]) show that the more closely members identified with each other and the team, the higher the team performance and the more learning that took place. On the other hand, other studies[17] suggest that a higher diversity in attitude towards the task is related to a greater amount of learning being experienced, especially in projects of relatively shorter duration; this is in turn associated with higher team performance.

There is now emerging a body of evidence that suggests that organisations' diversity objectives can best be delivered not by structural or policy change, but by creating the opportunities and tools for dialogue. In addition, the evidence points towards the team as the key location for this dialogue to take place. (Part of the success of diversity-focused mentoring relationships is that they form a small, mutual-learning-oriented team.) The implication for organizations is that it is important to shift resources from grandiose, company-wide initiatives towards the quality of learning dialogue among diverse teams.

Creating the environment for team learning

Diverse, psychologically safe environments don't just happen. They are the result of positive assumptions about the team and other members, and of attitudes that emphasize a willingness to learn and to help others to learn. In particular, people need to feel that:

◆ Mistakes are an opportunity for learning, not a source of blame.
◆ Everyone's ideas are valued.
◆ When it comes to reviewing process, everyone is an expert, even if only in the steps that concern their job role.
◆ Enquiry into other members' feelings and perspectives is encouraged.
◆ Everyone has a right and a responsibility to question what they do not understand or what they think may not be right.
◆ Curiosity is a virtue.

- Asking for help is welcomed; admitting ignorance is a sign of strength, not weakness.
- Learning is a shared responsibility.

When team members feel positive about these issues, they are more likely to experiment, both individually and as a team; to confront dysfunctional behaviours and poor work processes; to draw learning into the team from outside; and to apply learning to improving the task.

LEARNING IN A CARDIAC TEAM

A good example of this process at work is a study of cardiac surgery teams in the US,[18] which were switching to a new, complex procedure that replaced open-heart surgery with a less invasive approach, in which the surgeon operates through a relatively small incision near the ribs. Each member of the team had to learn new tasks that went contrary to the well-rehearsed routines they had previously used. Roles changed, too, with several members of the team now responsible for communication. In the 16 cardiac teams studied, all initially took between two and three times longer for the new operation compared to the previous procedure, because they had to check each step meticulously. All the 16 teams had been through exactly the same training, so the researchers had an opportunity to compare closely what factors influenced how rapidly the teams learned to reduce the operation time.

Some of the results were surprising and counter-intuitive. Things that didn't have any significant influence on the steepness of the learning curve included:

- Differences in educational background or length of surgical experience

- High-level management support for the team and its project

- The status of the surgeon leading the team

- Debriefs, project audits and after-action reports

What *did* make a difference was how the teams were designed and managed, in terms of both the task and the learning. In the teams that adapted fastest to the new routines, the leaders (the surgeons) selected team members not just on their technical ability, but also on their "ability to work with others, willingness to deal with new and ambiguous situations and confidence in offering suggestions to team members with higher status". The successful teams were also the most stable – the high degree of interdependence of task meant that newcomers were disruptive. In effect, these teams were designed for learning. (A similar effect has been noted where organizations introduce flexible working patterns: the teams that are most productive under the new routines are not existing teams that have taken on the procedures, but stable new teams whose members learn together.)

The successful teams also had leaders who presented the new procedures as "an organizational challenge rather than a technical one". They emphasized new ways of working together as a team, rather than the acquisition of new skills by individuals. These leaders made the learning process exciting by being positive about the benefits to patients; and by recognizing and accommodating stress within the team.

In addition, the successful teams and their leaders created an atmosphere of psychological safety. They experimented constantly, engaging in "real-time learning" – analysing and drawing lessons from the process while it was underway. The leaders of these teams made it clear that they were on a learning curve, too; and that the members were selected not just because of their skills, but because of their ability to comment on and improve the process.

The researchers' conclusion is that "teams learn more quickly if they are explicitly managed for learning". Their results also support the essential interaction between focus on task, learning and behaviour. Of course, this study is based on only one type of team; however, the lessons provide at the very least a starting point for thinking about the dynamics of learning in other types of team.

Six types of team for learning

Two factors that appear to have a significant impact on the team's ability to learn are the stability of membership and the stability of task. New faces are new learning resources; new tasks provide learning opportunities. However, if newcomers and their ideas are not valued, or if new tasks are approached in the same way as previous tasks, that learning potential may not be realized. The matrix in Figure 4.5 distinguishes six types of team by virtue of where they fit against these two dimensions of stability and change.

Stable teams perform the same task, or variations of it, over a long period, with relatively stable membership. They can be very cosy places to work: there are few surprises, everyone knows what is expected of them and there is an established set of internal rules, norms and shared assumptions. These teams can also be hotbeds of hidden stress, as people hide their concerns to avoid open conflict. Weak members may be protected by colleagues who work round them and compensate for their ineffectiveness. The skills required in a stable team are therefore heavily biased towards maintaining social cohesion. The typical problems relate to lack of change and a decreasing ability or inclination to challenge the status quo. Recent research into the level and quality of creativity in teams found that it increased significantly when new members joined and stagnated in teams that did not have occasional changes in membership.[19]

"Hit" or project teams are set up to deal with relatively short-term, usually one-off tasks, with members typically drawn from

FIGURE 4.5

SIX TYPES OF TEAM

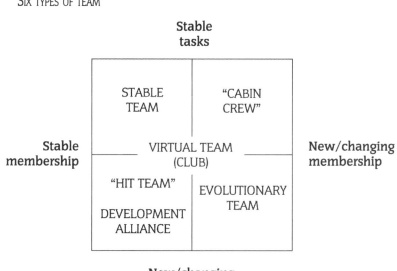

several other teams. Typically the membership is relatively stable, but as the team deals successfully with one task it is asked to deal with others. For example, a change team set up to deal with the introduction of a major piece of new technology developed a composite set of skills and processes that made it ideal to oversee first a restructuring of a corporate function and subsequently a number of other culture change initiatives. Although new faces did join the team at each point, the core membership remained the same. The skills involved in hit teams relate to the ability to adapt rapidly to new challenges and to deliver innovative outcomes to tight deadlines. Hit teams often face difficulties in integrating different skill sets and in interfacing with the larger organization.

Development alliances are composed of two or more people not necessarily linked within a normal team, who agree to share learning, for example offline mentoring or an action learning team. The skills required here include the ability to conduct learning dialogue and to manage self-development. Problems for development alliances include the difficulty of allocating time to a non-task activity.

"**Cabin crew**" have high stability of task, but low stability of membership. The obvious example is the cabin crew on a commercial aircraft, but others include film crews and actors. In each case, team members have to slot into their roles with minimal instruction or supervision, even though they may never have worked with each other before. The skills demanded in this type of team include high personal competence in a clearly defined technical task and an ability to link in swiftly and smoothly with the group activity. Problems for cabin crew include the difficulty of developing social cohesion among a continuous flow of strangers.

Evolutionary teams tackle longer-term developmental projects, such as the design and launch of a major new product or the establishment of a greenfield factory site. Their membership is relatively fluid, with members entering and leaving as the task changes according to the stage the project has reached. Skills here include being able to be creative in managing the new task, while being constrained by the decisions and processes introduced by previous members, who may or may not still be with the team. Problems for evolutionary teams include managing the handover between members working on different stages of the project.

Finally, **virtual teams** or **club teams** may be stable or unstable in both membership and task. Typically off the radar of the organizational chart, these teams consist of people who are pulled together by an influential manager on an *ad hoc* basis from scattered locations (virtual teams) or who coalesce independently (club teams). The members almost always have a second, more immediate role in another team type. There are many similarities between these teams and networks, but what differentiates them from a network is the presence of a clear sense of mutual purpose (for example to change the organization's thinking on work–life balance or on diversity issues) and a degree of clarity about tasks and roles. These teams may evolve from networks or into networks, as the urgency of their objectives changes. Skills for operating in this type of team include maintaining effective communication over distance or simply with people who are not part of one's routine work interactions, managing conflicting priorities, and ensuring that tasks and schedules are clearly understood. Problems for virtual and club teams include maintaining quality, sustaining motivation and coordinating complex tasks.

The typical description of a virtual team is one where the members are geographically separated and communicate primarily by electronic means. It isn't quite that simple, however. For example, the members of a senior management team in a manufacturing multinational are all based in the same building. Yet they all travel so much that less than a quarter of them are likely to be there for their regular fortnightly team meetings. They manage by making those meetings virtual, using whatever technology is available wherever they are.

In other organizations, virtual teams refer primarily to groupings outside the normal reporting structure. People (who may or may not be in different locations) come together informally to tackle issues for which there is no formal arrangement; or are encouraged by the organization to form a pressure group, for example to promote diversity awareness. In both these cases, the virtuality stems not from geographical separation, although that may play a role, but from separation of reporting structure. At their most formal, such groups may have the characteristics of project teams; at their least formal, they may be no more than specialist networks.

Virtual teams may also vary considerably in their membership. In some cases the members are relatively permanent and it is clear, to the members at least, who is involved. In others, membership may change with the stage of a project and there may be core and peripheral members, who require different levels of interaction with each other and the team leader.

In short, virtual teams can take very different forms, but the dimensions that define them appear to be whether they:

◆　Are formal or informal
◆　Work within one or several reporting structures
◆　Work at a distance or close proximity in location

- Have stability of membership
- Have clarity of the team boundaries (who's in and not in)

THE TEAM LEARNING RESEARCH PROJECT

Our research into team learning was conducted in 1998 in three main phases, on behalf of Herts Training and Education Council (now trading as Exemplas) in the UK and funded by the European Community's Adapt programme. First, a literature search was carried out to identify any relevant previous studies and to provide background data to guide the questions asked in the field research. So little previous research was identified that a second search was carried out, which reconfirmed the paucity of relevant knowledge.

Secondly, companies within Hertfordshire were invited by letter to participate in the project, then companies from a wider region within the south and east of England. A total of 11 companies were selected, to represent as wide a mix as possible of public/private sector, company size and type of activity. The smallest company had fewer than 10 employees, the largest 500 (the local subsidiary of a multinational company employing 44,000 people).

Thirdly, focus group interviews were carried out in each company, the number depending on the size of the organization. Some groups were composed of natural stable teams; others were drawn from employees at random. As many types of team as possible were interviewed. The questions were aimed at gathering their perceptions of:

- How often they participated in or how familiar they were with each type of team

- Good and bad experience of learning in each type of team

- How much learning was planned, rather than incidental

◆ How each type of team captured and shared learning within the team and with other teams

Finally, after an initial analysis of the interview data, comments were invited from a range of companies (both those that had participated and others that had not) and other sources of expert opinion.

Learning in each of the six team types

Each of the six types of team has its own strengths and weaknesses from a learning perspective:

◆ **Stable teams** easily fall into routines where there is little stimulus to question how things are done. Only under crisis, normally externally generated, do they put great effort into learning, and sometimes not even then.

◆ **Hit teams** exist for such short periods that by the time they have gone through the maturing stages of getting to know and work with each other, they are disbanded and the learning acquired is scattered. The need for speed in resolving problems or making things happen leaves little time for reflection and review of learning.

◆ **Evolutionary teams** suffer from the same learning difficulties as hit teams, but usually have the breathing space to reach maturity. They then meet a second set of learning problems in how they deal with newcomers. The original members have coalesced into a functioning team, and they have a strong shared experience and understanding of the values, principles and reasoning behind the way the project is being run. Newcomers find it difficult to join the club. All too often, there are two teams, insiders and outsiders, because the newcomers cannot catch up with the learning that the originals have undergone.

◆ **Virtual teams**, being mainly informal, rely on intuitive systems to ensure that learning takes place. Indeed, knowledge can be seen as the currency of the virtual team, so people with low levels of influence and experience may not be invited in. (This possibly explains why so few people at lower levels in organizations in our research had experience of working in virtual teams.)

◆ **Development alliances** have fewer inherent learning problems than other types of team, in part because their focus is already learning. The primary problems tend to revolve around what people learn in this mode. The attitudes, habits and behaviours of the more experienced partner will inevitably rub off, and not all of them may be helpful. Another frequently reported problem is insufficient frequency of interaction to make a significant difference.

◆ In **cabin crews**, the members meet infrequently, perhaps once only. Although the task remains the same and must be performed consistently (as with the cabin crew on an airplane), the membership changes frequently. This inhibits the potential for building learning relationships: there may be too little time to establish more than casual relationships. However, the variety of different people to learn from means that the observant person can acquire frequent tips and ideas that will build their base of knowledge and skills. Some cabin crew team leaders make a point of spending time with younger members to pass on know-how, for example during aircraft stopovers or over meals between touring casts of players.

Coaching stable teams

Stable teams can benefit from coaching in many ways. Some of the most significant are described in this section.

TABLE 4.3

DRIVERS AND BARRIERS TO PERFORMANCE IN THE STABLE TEAM

STABLE TEAM	TASK ACHIEVEMENT	LEARNING ACHIEVEMENT	PRODUCTIVE BEHAVIOURS
Drivers	Familiarity with the task Division of roles according to skill and personal preference	Opportunity to get to know each other's strengths, experience, knowledge and skills Lasting coaching relationships develop between peers	Predictability Communication "shorthand"
Barriers	Social loafing Shielding of weak members Low creativity	Failure to question how things are done and why Most change is initiated from outside not within the team	Avoiding confronting dysfunctional behaviour Unwilling to change the status quo

Creating and maintaining the stimulus for challenging and reflecting on tasks, processes and relationships

Life in the stable team tends to establish its own routine. Whether that routine is comfortable or not depends on the degree and nature of stress induced within the team. When times are tough, people avoid challenging the assumptions to which they work, because doing so would mean they have to go through the potential trauma of change; when times are good, the stimulus to seek change-inducing insights is even feebler!

The team needs to create both reflective space and psychological safety if it is to overcome the inevitable forces of inertia. These may not be obvious; indeed, most of the time they are not. It is often the case, for example, that a team may be showing continuous signs of performance improvement (for example increasing sales or more units of production) without contributing significantly to its longer-term goals of, say, consolidating market share. In the expanding mobile telephone market, almost every company's sales teams thought they were doing a great job. When reality struck, under the guise of market saturation, many were taken completely by surprise. The coach can help the team find the time to look beyond business as usual, by agreeing times when the members will meet to think creatively about their goals and how they aim to achieve them.

The team coach can also help the team build in processes by which:

◆ Each team member is expected to provide, at least once every quarter, one significant challenge for themselves and one for the team.

◆ Opportunities are created for stakeholders, such as internal and external customers, to confront and challenge the team as a whole.

Recognizing and identifying the "elephant in the room"

The elephant in the room is a metaphor for what Daniel Goleman[20] calls "lacuna issues". People agree by silent consensus to leave a team member well alone because they are too difficult or painful to deal with. The need for social cohesion within the group can frequently lead to an unspoken collusion, in which behaviours by one or more team members are ignored by others for fear of "rocking the boat". They may create excuses (for example "these creative types are all prima donnas") or, in extremis, weave elaborate fictions to avoid confronting reality (for example "he contributes a great deal behind the scenes" to describe a non-executive director who had no understanding of the business, but was a golfing buddy of the chairman!).

The coach can help deal with the elephant in the room by encouraging the team to develop greater clarity of roles and responsibilities, along with more accurate, more relevant monitoring and feedback; by enabling it to discuss behavioural expectations and norms, along with developing agreed processes for constructive interpersonal feedback; and by challenging team members to explore their own behaviours and motivations and to seek feedback from colleagues.

Of course, the elephant in the room may not be a behavioural issue. It may be a task or process issue that the team is too afraid to address, for example the potential closure of their unit, or the possibility that an ageing fuel tank might leak and pollute the nearby river. The same principles apply. In addition, the coach can help the team build robust processes of risk analysis. Risk management in organizations is typically applied at a corporate or large-process level, such as construction of a plant or management of a hospital's clinical department. However, it has substantial application for teams in general.

Developing detailed process analyses provides the opportunity for dialogue within the team about the potential for problems to occur (estimated frequency) and the impact if they do occur. The coach can stimulate greater rigour in this dialogue than might otherwise be the case, making sure that all process steps are covered and that the team takes a realistic view of both potential frequency and potential impact. A key coaching question is: "What is our evidence for this estimate?"

Establishing the cycle of coaching intervention

The principles of time-based coaching interventions identified by Gersick (see Chapter 2) relate to project teams, where there is a clear start, mid and end point to the task. For the stable team, however, there is either one long-term, relatively unchanging task (for example a production line) or a series of similar but unique tasks (for example an editorial team). The coach can help the team design and identify routines that emulate the essential elements of the project team and so create the conditions under which the team can welcome and use different kinds of coaching interventions at each point.

To achieve this, the team needs to identify the natural pattern of work flow and the key cycles within it. In some stable teams, the nature of the work (for example where the team is managing several tasks in parallel, distributed among the members) may mean that part of the team is at one point in the cycle while the rest is at another. In this case, the coach encourages those who are at a different point in their own tasks to act as observers and commentators to their colleagues.

Putting greater depth and quality into communication systems and networks

Unlike most other forms of team, stable teams have the longevity to benefit from long-term investment in external networks. The coach can help the team consider the questions:

◆ What information do we need (or would help us) to be effective both on current and future tasks?

◆ What influence do we need to have outside of the team to allow us to do what is needed?

◆ Who are the key people with whom we need to build relationships in order to receive information and exert influence?

◆ What will make these people want to network with us? What can we offer them to make it worth their while?

◆ How well do we communicate with these people and with other stakeholders now? How do we know?

◆ How would they like us to communicate with them? How often?

◆ What can we do that will make their jobs easier?

◆ Who within the team has primary and secondary responsibility for maintaining each networking relationship?

Inducting new team members

New members of stable teams often find it hard to become accepted or to feel accepted. The longer the team has been established and the stronger the group norms, the harder it can be. New members typically either adjust their own behaviour and attitudes to fit that of the team, or move on. Yet the arrival of a new member is an excellent opportunity for renewing and revitalizing the team's identity, working practices, assumptions and vision.

The task for the coach is to help the team turn induction of a new member into a mutual learning opportunity. Key questions include:

◆ What does the new member need to know to become effective rapidly?

◆ What can the team do to extract the newcomer's knowledge, expertise and difference in perspective, before they become institutionalized into the team's ways of working?

◆ Where would a fresh pair of eyes be most helpful in reviewing our processes?

A useful device is to put aside some time at a team meeting in the newcomer's first few weeks to discuss their top ten naïve questions. Not only does this encourage the newcomer to ask such questions and so speed their own learning, but it obliges the team to acknowledge the value of a naïve perspective.

Going bananas

A Dutch team with which I have worked instituted the practice of "banana memos", based on the story of how monkeys newly introduced to a social environment are made to conform to apparently illogical rules.

In the story, three monkeys are placed in a cage, and a bunch of bananas hangs from the top of a dead tree. When one attempts to climb the tree, all the monkeys are drenched with cold water. After a couple of experiences of drenching, the monkeys avoid the tree. When one monkey is removed and replaced, the newcomer also wants to climb the tree, but is forcibly persuaded not to by the others. More monkeys are replaced and eventually none of the monkeys in the cage has experienced the drenching, but the rule about not climbing the tree is so firmly ingrained in the social norms that the bananas remain untouched, through several generations of substitutions.

Banana memos can come from any member of staff, but are especially encouraged from employees in their first six months. They usually involve a question: Why do we do this? Or why don't we do that? The process owner – or the team as a whole, as appropriate – is obliged to take the question seriously and to try to view it through the neophyte's eyes. The process has made the team review and modify procedures that had been created for one, historical set of circumstances and remained "the way we do it" in spite of changes in the team's role and internal customer base.

Useful general coaching questions for stable teams include:

- How can we combat complacency?
- Are we really as good as we think we are? (Remember, teams instinctively overrate their own ability and other positive characteristics vis-à-vis the competition.)
- How much social loafing is occurring and what should we do about it?
- What naïve questions should we be asking ourselves regularly and who will do so?

Coaching cabin crew teams

The first problem a coach encounters within a cabin crew team is finding the team. Because the members come together in potentially unique combinations each time, the focus of learning has to be around building individual competences to slot in and contribute in each new assignment; or on creating learning opportunities within the confines of a single assignment.

Coaches working with air crew have used the pre-flight briefings and post-flight social wind-downs as *ad hoc* coaching opportu-

TABLE 4.4

DRIVERS AND BARRIERS TO PERFORMANCE IN THE CABIN CREW TEAM

CABIN CREW TEAM	TASK ACHIEVEMENT	LEARNING ACHIEVEMENT	PRODUCTIVE BEHAVIOURS
Drivers	Clearly defined, transparent routines	Multiple people to learn from	Expertise in own role and in collaboration with strangers
Barriers	Relative avoidance of *ad hoc* experimentation	Difficulty of building long-term relationships Training usually done outside the team Narrowness of task (tasks have to be relatively simple and repetitive to maintain quality and consistency)	Role protectiveness may be divisive

nities. They also seek to pair up experienced and less experienced team members. More value comes from the latter when a specific learning goal is identified. For example, "If we have a difficult customer, Jenny will deal with them, but you assist and observe." Finding the time to review the learning afterwards isn't easy (and the crew may be too tired at the end of a long-haul flight to take it in), but it seems that the sooner coachees can articulate to colleagues what they have learned, the more readily the learning will "stick".

In cabin crew teams with longer duration, such as a theatre cast or a film crew, coaching can also educate the learner about the range of other roles that they support and/or depend on. Again, an important role for the team coach is to encourage and underpin learning relationships between old hands and less experienced members, or between peers from different disciplines.

The most difficult task for the coach working with this type of team is to help it examine and challenge its basic processes and routines. Because each new team has to gel instantly, the norms of behaviour, processes and roles tend to be vocationally determined. Even if one team experiments and does things differently, a week later its members will be back into teams that do things the traditional way. Experimentation tends, therefore, to be confined to individual creativity, for example in how to interpret a part, or how to comfort an unhappy child passenger. Organizations employing lots of cabin crew teams sometimes overcome this problem by

TABLE 4.5

DRIVERS AND BARRIERS TO PERFORMANCE IN THE PROJECT TEAM

PROJECT TEAM	TASK ACHIEVEMENT	LEARNING ACHIEVEMENT	PRODUCTIVE BEHAVIOURS
Drivers	Narrow focus of activity Opportunities to experiment Relatively short duration between concept and outcomes	Diverse expertise to learn from Process conflict can be positive Brings people into a different team environment High need to acquire and apply knowledge rapidly	Recognition of expertise
Barriers	Task ownership is distributed	Lack of time to develop learning relationships Failure to capture learning – team dissolves before it can achieve learning maturity Time pressure to complete the task puts review of learning on the back burner	Lack of time to develop cohesive work routines and social norms

selecting one or two teams as pilots (no pun intended!), building reflective space into their schedules for review, analysis and task adaptation.

Coaching project teams

Project teams respond best to different types of intervention at different points in their life cycle.[21] The coach's role is to help the team focus on the right things at the right time.

When the team forms, the coach can guide it towards clarifying goals (developing a common sense of purpose and priorities around both task and learning objectives), identifying the scope and location of team knowledge, establishing the basic systems of communication and coordination, and developing expectations of roles and behaviours.

At the mid point, the coach can ensure that the team has the opportunities to draw breath and reflect on process, communication and relationships, and to revisit the team strategy. Finally, towards the end of the project, the coach can encourage the team to reflect on the learning it has achieved and how it will capture and disseminate it.

Coaching questions for **clarifying goals** include:

- What is the context in which this project was conceived?
- Why does it matter? To whom?
- What specifically are the task goals? The learning goals? Are they SMART (specific, measurable, attainable, realistic and tangible)?
- What will success look like?
- What would failure look like?
- How will we know how well we have done on both task and learning goals?
- How do our individual goals fit with the collective goals?
- What would prevent us achieving the goal?
- What are the five key things we have to get right to achieve the goal?

Coaching questions for **identifying the scope and location of team knowledge** include:

◆ Why was *this* team selected? What specific skills and knowledge do we bring individually? What skills and knowledge does each of us have access to?

◆ What knowledge does the team need? What is core (can't do without)? What is valuable (will make the task easier)? What is potentially useful (may need to draw on if certain situations or needs arise)?

◆ What knowledge is explicit (i.e. captured in a way that others can access) and what is tacit (held in people's minds)? How will we access the latter when we need it?

◆ Are there identifiable knowledge gaps? How will we plug these?

Coaching questions for **establishing the basic systems of communication and coordination** include:

◆ Who do we need to inform, consult and invite to participate in decisions and in key stages of each team process?

◆ How do they expect the communication to occur?

◆ What lessons can we learn from past communication failures?

◆ Are we aware of each other's communication styles?

◆ Where do we need to make a special effort to communicate?

◆ If the team is scattered, how frequently do we need to have formal communications to maintain our focus?

◆ Have we got the balance right between transactional communication (task related) and relationship-building communication? (Again, particularly important for project teams whose members do not work together.)

BALANCING RELATIONAL AND TRANSACTIONAL COMMUNICATION

An employee communication company called item had purchased a competitor and decided to move all its operations into the acquired company's premises in London. This increased the number of staff who worked from home all or much of the time.

Staff who continued to work from the office had to learn to spend telephone time with the home workers, keeping them up to date socially as much as possible to the level that would occur through regular and frequent meetings in the staff kitchen. Relational communication proved as important as transactional communication in maintaining the motivation of the home workers and the mutual trust between the two groups of the same team.

Coaching questions for **developing expectations of roles and behaviours** include:

- What expertise does each of us bring?
- What expertise does each of us want to develop?
- What behaviours will support and hinder the achievement of the team goals? What is our process for flagging up behaviours that don't help and giving due credit for behaviours that do?
- How can we be sure that we use our collective expertise most productively?
- Who is responsible for which processes?
- Which decisions or communications to the outside world require consultation and with whom?

Coaching questions for **reflection on process, communication and relationships** include:

- Did we do this the best way possible, so far?
- Which elements of the process are most vulnerable?
- What could have been better communicated and how?
- How effective were we at managing conflict? (Was there enough positive conflict?)
- What can we do to improve the process, communication and relationships?

- Do we have as much or more enthusiasm for the project as at the beginning? If not, what do we need to change and how will we do that?
- What issues do we need to tackle in terms of resources?

Coaching questions for **revisiting strategy** include:

- What did and didn't work?
- What has changed in the environment in which we operate?
- What has changed within the team?
- What assumptions do we want to challenge about what we are doing and why?
- What changes do we want to make to our scenarios of success?

Coaching questions for **reflection on learning** include:

- What has changed in our individual and collective knowledge, our self-awareness, our perception of reality?
- What have we learned about the process of team formation?
- How have we used this learning? (What have we done with it?)
- What is our process for capturing and sharing this learning?
- How can we make sure it is available to others?
- How will we build on this learning?
- What can we do to continue to learn from each other once the project team is disbanded?

Project teams as vehicles for learning

Although learning alliances are the only team types specifically designed for learning, project and evolutionary teams are often the most fruitful sources of organizational learning. A key element in the effectiveness of these teams, it can be argued, is how they draw on and pull together knowledge already held, create new knowledge and redistribute that knowledge back into the organization. We can describe these three processes as **gathering**, **synthesis** and **redistri-**

FIGURE 4.6

FIGURE 4.6

LEARNING IN PROJECT TEAMS

bution (see Figure 4.6). The danger, as in all team types, is that so much attention is paid to achieving the primary task that these opportunities for learning are either lost, or one or more steps is omitted. The more effective the project team is in managing the learning task, the more it can contribute to organizational knowledge and hence to longer-term capability.

In theory, the ideal project team brings together a team of experts, who have between them all the requisite knowledge to manage and complete the task. In practice, designing project teams in this way undermines the effectiveness of all three stages. Experts tend to rely on their own knowledge, rather than investing time and effort in finding out what other knowledge exists. While they may learn from each other during the synthesis phase, they have often developed routines, if they have worked together frequently, that shut out radical alternatives. And because they are less excited about new knowledge that has been generated, they invest less in disseminating that knowledge.

HOW NOT TO LEARN IN A PROJECT TEAM

An international oil company was under intense pressure to speed up the pace of indigenization in one of its developing-nation oil fields. It had a willing pool of well-educated young engineers and managers, who were intended eventually to take the places of expatriates, but their progress into the relevant positions was painfully slow. At the same time, the managing director had launched a cost-cutting initiative based on total quality, with over 200 project teams, ranging in size from two or three people to a dozen or more. The total quality programme was both urgent and important (at least to the company, though less so to the national government); the indigenization goal was important but less urgent, although everyone recognized that it was a time bomb ticking. As a result, the project teams were composed almost entirely of people who could contribute, rather than people who had the most to learn from exposure to the project process. Hence a major opportunity for learning was lost.

A more balanced approach to the situation would have been to include a number of local employees on each project team as understudies to the expatriate experts, who would have coached them by transferring specific knowledge and helping them gather information. This would have enriched the project discussions with more data about what was actually happening on the ground (as opposed to what the managers thought was happening). This intra-team coaching would also have enabled the local employees to understand the technical and business processes as they were analysed and dissected, and would have disseminated the knowledge rapidly within the organization.

Academic George Huber,[22] reviewing the literature on project teams and learning, examines these teams' dual roles as users and generators of organizational knowledge. He recommends that human resource policy should ensure that people are occasionally assigned to project teams, where they are virtually guaranteed to gain some new knowledge that will be value to their own task role in their normal team, or to their normal team as a whole.

Huber identifies three main barriers to knowledge transfer between teams of all kinds:

◆ **Absorptive capacity** – the team's ability to recognize the value of new, external information, assimilate it and apply it.[23] An important issue here is recognizing which members of the team are most open to specific areas of new knowledge and can thus be a knowledge conduit.

◆ **Causal ambiguity** – when it isn't clear why a team isn't performing well or a process isn't delivering. Remedies for this include effective processes of sharing knowledge and discussing problems within the team; and the exchange of formal "lessons learned" files between teams.

◆ **Arduous relationship** – the common situation, where sharing information is just too much trouble. Either the team members or the technology or the physical environment make it too difficult. People working in virtual project teams may, for example, need encouragement to note all the problems they encounter or all the good ideas they have for improvements. It's often easier just to plough on with the work. Having formal systems for capturing this knowledge on a frequent, simple basis and making people aware that their efforts are valued makes a considerable difference.

The opportunities for the team coach to intervene in all three of these circumstances are multiple. The goal once again, however, is to bring the team to the point where it can manage these barriers itself. In the case of project and evolutionary teams, which may be relatively short-lived, there is a case for coaching at the early stages to identify these barriers and help the team establish processes to overcome them.

Coaching evolutionary teams

Evolutionary teams are much more complicated than some of the other types, because there is effectively a new team every time the project moves to a fresh phase. In essence, there are multiple beginnings, mid points and endings, but team members may be out of phase either with each other, or the overall process, or both. The

TABLE 4.6

DRIVERS AND BARRIERS TO PERFORMANCE IN THE EVOLUTIONARY TEAM

EVOLUTIONARY TEAM	TASK ACHIEVEMENT	LEARNING ACHIEVEMENT	PRODUCTIVE BEHAVIOURS
Drivers	Just-in-time injection of expertise, in the form of new members	Often have more time to reflect, due to the long-term nature of projects Exposure to a variety of tasks, perspectives and knowledge pools	"Mobile diversity" – the team structure obliges people to develop better ways of working with difference
Barriers	Process handovers may be dislocated by loss of knowledge or expertise	Difficult for each wave of new members to catch up and understand prior team learning	The team often operates as several teams within a team, with little discussion about learning between them

role of the team coach, in addition to those of the project team coach, is therefore to help the team achieve continuity, absorbing new phases and new members relatively seamlessly.

The keys to doing this lie in helping the team make tacit knowledge explicit, value new and past contributions, and recognize and manage phase transitions.

Making tacit knowledge explicit

Newcomers to any established team face a period of acclimatization, during which they become socialized into the team's way of doing things or are rejected by the team's immune system. Much of the knowledge absorbed in this way is instinctive, intuitive and implicit. It can also be based to a large extent on assumptions and half-truths. The coach can help the team and the newcomer manage this process so that:

- The newcomer understands how the collective wisdom and norms evolved.
- The acclimatization process is two way, with the team learning from the newcomer.
- Assumptions about what is good practice are surfaced and tested frequently.
- The thinking behind procedures and decision making is shared and explored.

For this to happen, the team dialogue needs to focus on the evolution of context (what happened to shape our approach to an issue), ideas (where and how we tried to innovate) and judgement (the more or less systematic thinking applied to making choices and decisions and the assumptions underlying the decision-making process).

One coaching technique that works well in this situation is **retro-engineered learning**, in which the coach facilitates a dialogue between old hands and newcomers. The approach starts with the coach asking the old hands to describe the circumstances at the time the project began and the goals that were set. They then ask the newcomer(s) to say what they would have done in these circumstances and the assumptions that would have underlain their decisions. Next the old hands describe what actually happened and why, the mistakes they made and the constraints under which they operated. The newcomers are then given a chance to revise their description of what they would have done. The process continues as a cycle through a series of critical points until it reaches the current situation. Finally, the coach invites all the participants to:

- Identify what tacit learning has now become explicit.
- Question whether it is time to review any of the assumptions under which the team has been operating.

Valuing new and past contributions
Retro-engineered learning can also assist here, by helping newcomers understand the struggles and difficulties that earlier team

members encountered. In addition, the coach can use the techniques of appreciative inquiry to determine:

◆ What are the successes of each stage of this team's evolution?
◆ What valuable qualities have been introduced at each stage?
◆ What valuable qualities would the newcomers like to be recognized for?
◆ How can the team as a whole ensure that they are so recognized?
◆ What can we do together to repeat or build on the past successes?
◆ How will combining old and new perspectives help us achieve our goals better?

Recognizing and managing phase transitions

Sometimes people move in and out of evolutionary teams so fast that it seems there is no stability at all. But there will be underlying patterns as the team progresses from one project phase to the next, and it is at these points that the coach can add value by stimulating the team to pause and look both backwards and forwards. Phase transitions can sometimes be abrupt (e.g. agreement of funding or appointment of a new team leader) or gradual (e.g. step-by-step transfer of personnel to a new location), but they can be mapped.

Phase transition mapping in this context usually consists of two timelines: one relating to the task itself and one relating to the inflow and outflow of key people or expertise. Developing a phase transition map with the team creates a dialogue about when would be good times to start anew, review progress and extract learning. The more these interventions are predicted and prepared for, the easier is the task of both the coach and the team.

Coaching virtual teams

Virtual teams come in two types: those that are virtual because of where people are located (Type A); and those that are virtual in the

TABLE 4.7

DRIVERS AND BARRIERS TO PERFORMANCE IN THE TYPE A VIRTUAL TEAM

TYPE A VIRTUAL TEAM: GEOGRAPHICALLY SCATTERED	TASK ACHIEVEMENT	LEARNING ACHIEVEMENT	PRODUCTIVE BEHAVIOURS
Drivers	Continuous working (with transcontinental projects) Diversity of expertise, perspective (and sometimes culture)	Exchange of information and learning is a key currency of the network Diversity of membership (typically) – often extending outside the organization	Relational communication
Barriers	Communication breakdowns Tendency to put more immediate projects first Balancing technical and interpersonal skills Greater difficulty of achieving synergy	Difficulty of getting timely feedback	Lack of verbal clarity Problems in building trust at a distance Isolation and detachment Difficulties in assessing and recognizing performance

sense of being informal networks of influence (Type B). Each type has its own issues around task learning and behaviour, as shown in Tables 4.7 and 4.8.

The coach working with Type A virtual teams can broadly treat it as a project team with limited or no opportunities for physical meetings. All of the activities and interventions relevant to coaching the project team apply, but in addition, the coach can help the team recognize, understand and manage the more complex communication and motivational issues.

TABLE 4.8

DRIVERS AND BARRIERS TO PERFORMANCE IN THE TYPE B VIRTUAL TEAM

TYPE B VIRTUAL TEAM: THE "CLUB" TEAM	TASK ACHIEVEMENT	LEARNING ACHIEVEMENT	PRODUCTIVE BEHAVIOURS
Drivers	Political linkages can exert influence over resources and policies	Exchange of information and learning is a key currency of the network	Willingness to provide practical support and learning in the pursuit of a common goal
Barriers	Lack of clear leadership and boundaries Lack of "official" status means the team can be subverted by other interest groups Lack of clarity about when the team's task is finished	Lack of formal learning objectives As easy for people to be excluded as included through "exclusive" nature of the team	Members can be diverted by individual priorities and deadlines

The authors of *Mastering Virtual Teams*[24] describe a number of competences that virtual team members need, all of which are suitable topics to address through both individual and team coaching. They determine that team members need skills of:

◆ Project management
◆ Networking across functional, hierarchical and organizational boundaries
◆ Using communication and collaboration technologies effectively
◆ Setting personal boundaries and managing time
◆ Working across cultural and functional boundaries
◆ Using interpersonal awareness

Useful questions the coach can encourage the Type A virtual team to discuss include:

- Do we genuinely have the same understanding of the goals and priorities?
- What extra procedures or fail-safes do we need to ensure that everyone is aware of changes of context and/or thinking?
- How will we demonstrate respect and goodwill without physical meetings?
- How will we ensure that we listen to each other?
- How will we ensure that we all give the appropriate priority to this team when pressures are applied from our stable teams? What support can we provide each other when a conflict between the needs of these teams arises and how?
- How will we know if we are individually and collectively doing a good job?
- Which combinations of media will work best for each type of task or meeting?
- What rules do we need for managing online meetings? (Trying to use a virtual meeting for detailed work that should have been done via exchange of emails is a common mistake and one that causes people to dread their next encounter with their colleagues.)
- What rules do we need for *ad hoc* e-communications? (Netiquette includes rules such as not using capital letters, as these can be seen by the recipient as the equivalent of shouting!)
- What are our norms around key events, such as the induction of new members or preparation for virtual meetings?
- How will we develop and sustain a level of self-awareness and cultural awareness sufficient to recognize and surface potential or actual conflict?
- How will we make sure that everyone who should be part of the ongoing dialogue is included and that the way they give and receive information meets their preferences and local circumstances?

The team coach may also need to support the virtual team leader. Leading a virtual team is in many ways much more difficult than leading a normal team. You can't easily monitor what people are doing, or identify problems, except when people report in. Nor, in many cases, can you necessarily dictate when team members spend time on your project and on other people's.

Some of the key skills a virtual team leader requires include:

- **Motivating remotely**. It's very easy to forget that people are there and for them to feel neglected or uninformed. The effective virtual team leader invests time and effort in keeping contact, ensuring that at least some of the communication is relationship building rather than just transactional.
- **Getting things done through influence rather than authority**, especially when the members of the team also have other reporting lines through managers more local to them.
- **Maintaining focus** on both immediately urgent and long-term goals.
- **Managing behaviour**. When most communication is through electronic media, the potential for misunderstanding of each other's motives is high. In one multinational sales team, a few comments by a German to his Italian counterpart, intended to be helpful, were taken as a mortal offence. It took several months and a face-to-face meeting with the team leader as a facilitator to restore harmony within the team.
- **Appraising virtual performance**. The team leader needs to combine a high level of clarity of instruction and expectation with a review process that takes into account the very specific context in which each member is operating. In addition to assessing performance against absolute targets, the leader needs to help people understand how they are (or are not) contributing to helping their virtual team colleagues deliver against team deadlines and goals. This will often mean gathering data from team members about each other – a tricky task, if people are to be both honest and non-defensive.

Especially for the inexperienced virtual team leader, coaching sessions may need to be relatively frequent, depending on the timescale of the project. The lack of "normal" interaction between members means that the potential for team characteristics to atrophy is much higher; encouraging members to reflect together frequently counteracts these tendencies towards entropy. As with any other team type, however, the coach should judge their own success in part by how rapidly the team takes over the coaching functions itself. (See Chapter 6 for more on this.)

Type B virtual teams have different issues and require a different approach. Just getting them all to take part in reflective activity is a challenge in Type A, but even more so in Type B. Indeed, outsiders may not even know who the members are. There seems to be very little recorded experience of coaching this type of team. In my own experience, the coaching sessions come about under some other guise, such as a series of briefings. There is always a small group of core sponsors, typically budget holders, who recognize the value of an informal team in working within the walls of the organization and who are convinced that the organization needs to change some part of its culture, technology or strategy.

Some of the critical questions the coach can put in this situation include:

- How much of a team do we want/need to be?
- How will we ensure that we have a common goal and priorities?
- How committed are we to the goal? (What sacrifices are we prepared to make to bring it about?)
- How inclusive/exclusive do we want to be? (Sometimes a small, focused group can accomplish more than a large, open group, and vice versa.)
- What responsibilities do we want to have towards each other?
- How open do we want to be about our task?
- How subversive do we want to be in respect of the prevailing corporate culture?

- What are the risks and opportunities of being part of an informal team in general? And of this team in particular?
- How will we make sure that the team makes progress? (Who sets and monitors deadlines?)
- What systems do we need to maintain our informality yet be effective in achieving our task?
- How can we sustain the team for the long haul, if we need to?

Measuring the results of coaching interventions with "club teams" is difficult. The fact that they operate in the shadows means that their achievements are often indirect and through influence; it also sometimes takes years before the full effects are felt. In this case, the coach may need to focus more on process and learning outcomes than on organizational impact.

An international virtual team

In the world of fast-moving consumer goods, retailing pharmaceuticals is one of the most competitive marketplaces. The pharmaceuticals division of a multinational company was trying to establish a more joined-up campaign strategy across countries in order to improve sales and profitability. There were many barriers to this, for example duplicated or unclear roles among senior people and the structure of the company, in which budgets and accountabilities were devolved internationally. This meant that there was no incentive for country heads to pay attention to anything other than their own fiefdom. Previous efforts to address this issue had taken a really long time for little result.

There were six country sales managers managing campaigns and personnel internationally with teams of between 20 and 50 people. They worked to a matrix management structure (they reported to a country manager as well as to the global head of campaigns). The sales managers had not responded at all to the global head of campaigns, who was understandably getting very frustrated and was not going to accept this for much longer. They had met as a group twice before, but felt that these meetings were a waste of time and should be abandoned. They simply did not have any interest in working together.

The company brought in an experienced coach, Sharon Bajer from leadership development consultancy SKAI Associates, who had experience working with dysfunctional groups, particularly across international boundaries where there were distinct cultural differences as well as the obvious time-zone and working practice challenges. She began by observing a team session and giving the group feedback, on areas such as the business implications of the parent–child behaviours exhibited in the group. The team then asked SKAI for further help in setting out better ways of working, goals and roles, and generally improving their group working skills.

Bajer ran three quarterly coaching sessions with the team. The first was designed to help the team establish what they existed for and how they were going to work. This session transferred responsibility away from the leader to the group members. They helped design the session and had to facilitate part of it (with a small amount of facilitation skills training). The second session addressed the same area in more depth, with more facilitation skills training. The third session focused on communication skills, which were particularly important because the team's communication was very undisciplined, took ages and was enormously frustrating for everyone.

The outcome was the creation of an effective self-managed team, which meant that much less time was required by the leader. The team members now felt that there was a good return on the investment of time they spent with each other. Two members were promoted. The team was able to get through at least three times more work than previously. The working climate changed from bored and petulant to dynamic, creative and businesslike. Some team members have taken the process back to their national units to replicate it.

Written by SKAI Associates, www.skai.co.uk.

Coaching learning alliances

Learning alliances come in several forms, but the most common (apart from one-to-one coaching or mentoring relationships) are action learning sets, learning clubs and group mentoring.

Action learning is a well-established process that relates learning to current, meaningful tasks, on which learners receive the benefit of support, criticism and *ad hoc* coaching from each other. The members do not normally work together – they may be drawn from different parts of the same organization or from a variety of different organizations – but they tend to be peers, in terms of experience and/or organizational level. Most action learning sets start off with the aid of a facilitator/coach, who helps the team members become familiar with the processes of collaborative enquiry, but effective action learning usually aims to equip the team to manage its own learning processes in due course.

The role of the action learning coach, then, is to help the group become self-sufficient. The role may well start off as facilitation, with the coach introducing the process, setting the ground rules and acting as master of ceremonies in the ensuing dialogue. The coach will also at this stage typically provide some knowledge input and conceptual frameworks that team members can use to understand and analyse the issues and projects they bring to the learning dialogue, and provide one-to-one coaching as needed. As the team gradually takes greater control of the process, the team coaching role becomes increasingly less important, eventually to the point where the team facilitates itself and the coach concentrates on assisting the quality of their thinking. The coach's role is then at an end and they can withdraw gracefully.

TABLE 4.9

DRIVERS AND BARRIERS TO PERFORMANCE IN THE LEARNING ALLIANCE

LEARNING ALLIANCE TEAM	TASK ACHIEVEMENT	LEARNING ACHIEVEMENT	PRODUCTIVE BEHAVIOURS
Drivers	Goal is owned by the individual	Focused on learning rather than task achievement High potential for mutual learning (two for one) Often just-in-time learning	Open dialogue and enquiry
Barriers	Learning may not be sufficiently closely linked to work task	Organization culture may discourage spending time on "non-productive" activities Many managers lack the skills and/or inclination to become effective coaches or mentors	Lack of knowledge of each other's specific job role and team circumstances

Learning clubs are an evolution of what used to be called reading circles. Members come together regularly to discuss new ideas that they have encountered in reading and the implications of those ideas for their own development, for their practice as managers or professionals, or for the organization. In some cases, everyone reads the same book or sections of a book; in others, people read different parts of the same book, so that their contributions can be complementary. Again, the role of the coach is to help them extract the most they can from the ideas considered.

Typical coaching themes in this context include:

- How to analyse and evaluate ideas in a text
- How to present ideas to the group as a whole
- How to generate the questions that will open up debate and dialogue
- How to ensure that learning is applied

GROUP MENTORING BASED ON TEAM LEARNING

When the Crown Solicitor's Office (CSO) in South Australia was undergoing major change, people felt isolated and trapped in their sections, particularly if they were geographically isolated. The CEO funded a steering group, initiated and managed by a senior lawyer and including junior and senior, professional and non-professional staff, to create a preferred workplace for talented staff. As part of the initiative, a mentoring programme based on team learning provided a framework for exploring key business issues, such as strategic direction and how to achieve a workplace that would value people and embrace change.

The steering group identified at the beginning a variety of issues that team mentoring could address. Among them were:

- How can we value people better?

- What do we have to do to be professional?

- What motivates people across generations?

- How do I get promoted around here?

- How do we rejuvenate the workplace?

Initially there was a degree of scepticism about the mentoring initiative and whether it would lead to worthwhile outcomes or become merely a "talk fest". There was also some concern that senior management would not support it. Many said that they didn't know what to expect and that it cut across all of their previous notions of mentoring.

Anticipated expectations on the part of the organizers were:

◆ Mentoring and coaching would become an integral part of the organization's culture.

◆ Senior lawyers/managers would share their expertise with others.

◆ Strong collaborative support networks would form.

◆ Knowledge and skills would be shared across sections.

Two mentoring circles were formed, with seven participants in each. They met, with a team coach/facilitator, every three weeks for six months. Each person in the circle was invited to lead a conversation or discussion on a topic that the members had chosen. Before the session the team coach spent an hour with that person supporting the structure of the conversation, helping with resources and suggesting process; afterwards they gave personal feedback. This provided an opportunity for one-on-one coaching and ensured that the team members took over the ownership of the process. The role of the coach during the meeting included helping to keep the conversation focused, challenging paradigms, and ensuring clarity of purpose and equal participation. The coach additionally met with all members individually at least once during the six-month period.

The assumptions that the programme incorporated included:

◆ Knowledge is created when organizational members interact with each other through dialogue.

◆ Communication is improved when people from diverse ages and backgrounds hold conversations with each other in order to share meanings.

◆ Change initiatives work when there is ownership at all organizational levels.

◆ Diversity (gender, experience, age, skills) is important to the success of teams.

Individual and group goals were set by the participants at the beginning and reinforced by the facilitator/coach throughout the team meetings. A peer-mentoring guide was prepared and helped to guide the group process.

The results were far better than anticipated: 100% attendance, with mentoring circle members wanting to continue to meet beyond the anticipated scheduled programme. Innovative ideas for changing the workplace culture became the topic of recommendations to senior management and have since formed part of the basis for the new strategic directions of CSO. Many of these changes are now being implemented. Additionally, a snowball effect occurred, with 30 additional lawyers joining the mentoring programme. One of the original groups has been meeting regularly with the coach to learn how to coach/facilitate future mentoring circles.

Learning reviews occurred at the end of each session, with suggestions for improvement of the process. A formal evaluation occurred at the end of the first year. Success was largely measured by attendance and people's enthusiasm to continue meeting after the initial programme.

On the downside, only four of the 40 participants over the past few years are in senior management positions. Additionally, only four are non-lawyers, indicating perceived boundaries between staff and management/professional and administrative staff. People are keen to address these issues in future activities.

The biggest challenges for the team were managing time and achieving consistency of attendance; for the coach, the constant challenge was to help the participants challenge their thinking and paradigms. The greatest learning for the team lay in practising communication skills, receiving feedback and solving real problems, along with how to support each other.

Individuals learned more about themselves and how to work within the organization. They gained confidence and increased awareness of themselves and others. The other party in the learning was the coach, who reported that the discussions had created insights into how to balance time, space and boundaries.

Often someone brought along a work-based problem and mentoring circle members helped them reflect, share experiences and work out a plan of action to implement in the workplace. Others wanted the group to give an opinion on a new policy or procedure and members were challenged to look beyond the immediate solution. Many became active in bringing about cultural change within the organization.

Written by Dr Ann Darwin, the team coach for these mentoring circles and the principal consultant and managing director of Ann Darwin & Associates, based in Adelaide. Her email address is adarwin@ozemail.com.au.

The team learning process

In our study of learning processes in different types of team, we discovered that there is, indeed, a process that teams that are perceived and perceive themselves to be good at learning adopt. As is so often the case, the process is a cycle (see Figure 4.7 overleaf).

The cycle starts with clarity about the goals for learning. From current research into learning alliances, it seems that there is a clear relationship between how specific learning goals are and how well they are achieved. Commitment of the learner also plays a part.

Let's take each of the steps in turn.

Setting the goals for learning

Team learning goals are where individual and organizational goals meet. Critical questions here are:

FIGURE 4.7

THE TEAM LEARNING PROCESS

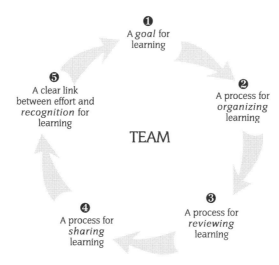

- What knowledge, skills and behaviours does the team need to achieve the task goals it has been set – now, in the next 12 months, over a longer period?
- Are we clear how those capabilities will help us achieve the organizational goals?
- What is the current level of knowledge, skills and behaviour in this context?
- If there is a gap, how big is it?
- Which gaps need to be addressed by learning on behalf of the team as a whole, and which need to be focused on individuals? (Some gaps may relate to inexperience on the part of some team members, for example in areas where everyone needs to be effective; others may relate to competences required by only a few people in the team, depending on the roles they play.)
- What are our resources for bridging the gap, both internally and externally? (For example, external resources might include training or delegating tasks to someone outside the team; internal resources might include co-coaching.)

Learning goals can arise from a wide range of sources, but the two most common arise from internal ambition and external feedback. Effective teams develop a collective ambition that encompasses both what the team does and its identity. Success isn't normally associated with teams that aspire to be "no worse than our competitors". Articulating the team's ambition, its underlying values and implications, and how these all link into the corporate and individual aspirations and values, is an important part of the learning process. It provides a shared language for dialogue, lifts the vision of the team members beyond the day to day, and creates a touchstone for frequent reassessment of current task and learning activity against the broader and longer-term objectives of the team.

External feedback, at least when positive, reinforces the team ambition and therefore the commitment to learning goals. (It can, of course, also make the team complacent, if other processes are not present to maintain the momentum of learning.) There is evidence that teams respond to performance feedback by adjusting aspiration levels, in much the same way that individuals do.[25] Negative feedback creates opportunities for setting learning goals, but the team may first have to overcome the setback to its self-image and this depends to a significant extent on the team's resilience. Learning how to respond positively to negative feedback seems to be a core skill for the learning team.

Amy Edmondson suggests that organizations should construct teams with specific learning goals in mind. These teams would essentially become learning agents on behalf of the organization (the same principle can be applied to the individual as a learning agent for the team). Some of them would focus on incremental learning – improving existing routines and capabilities; others on radical learning – reframing situations, developing new capabilities, or solving ambiguous problems. Based on this analysis, it seems logical that teams should negotiate with their organization what externally initiated learning goals they should set. In our own work with teams over the past five years, we have found very few examples of teams actually doing this.

Organizing learning

Organizing learning takes this dialogue several steps further. It requires the team to develop and implement a **team learning plan**, a common understanding of learning needs and priorities, both collective and individual. In this context, the team learning plan is the bridge between the business plan and the employees' personal development plans. The plan details responsibilities, resources and timelines. In some cases, effective teams split collective learning tasks – such as how to improve the quality of marketing proposals – into sizeable chunks and give individuals the task of undertaking the relevant learning on behalf of the group. In a marketing example, the team concerned split the learning tasks into three elements: more accurate and timely feedback from customers, regaining lost customers and writing better proposals.

A key part of organizing learning is creating opportunities for reflection and reflective dialogue. Amy Edmondson,[26] again, has some useful insights. She distinguishes between learning behaviours that promote new insight (e.g. sharing information, discussing errors, seeking feedback and analysing past performance) and those that apply or use new insight (e.g. making decisions, changes and improvements, implementing new ideas and transferring information to others in the organization). The first category she describes as reflection, the second as change.

Teams that neither reflect nor initiate change are clearly not going to be very effective at learning. Teams that reflect but do not make changes as a result are probably wasting their time. Action may not occur because of inability to break out of routine, lack of resources, lack of motivation or many other reasons. Teams that make changes but don't reflect are likely to be relentlessly pursuing strategies and tactics that are well below optimum. In neither of these cases is the team likely to respond appropriately and in sufficient time to adapt their habitual routines to external stimuli.[27]

Teams that both reflect and initiate change exhibited several common characteristics in Edmondson's study. First, there was little evidence of power distance. Team leaders made very little use of their authority or status, encouraging open discussion and consensus. They took care not to overrule team members. Secondly, they organized the work so that members were substantially interdependent. By contrast, teams that didn't implement change tended to be those where the work was structured to allow team members to operate relatively independently. Thirdly, goals in the teams that both reflected and changed were more explicit and people's actions were informed by objective data, rather than nuance and inference. In the less effective teams – all of which had less psychological safety – implicit goals that ran contrary to the formal goals took precedence in shaping behaviours. For example, members of one team were content to wait for someone else to sort out production problems, because the backlog would need to be made up through lucrative overtime.

Some practical processes for organizing learning include:

◆ Breaking up complex tasks into chunks, each of which can be owned by one or two individuals. They have the responsibility not only to undertake the learning on behalf of the team, but to ensure that it is integrated with all the other relevant learning, both past and present.
◆ Establishing reading circles, where teams select a different book or article to discuss at each regular meeting.
◆ Setting aside specific times for learning.
◆ Assigning experienced team members to coach the less experienced.

Coaching questions for organizing learning include:

◆ What learning won't happen unless someone makes it happen?
◆ Who is responsible for what aspects of the team's collective knowledge and skills?
◆ How will we know when relevant learning is taking place?

◆ What can we do to manage the pace of learning?
◆ How can we link individual and collective learning?
◆ How can we create learning opportunities and make sure that we take full advantage of them?

Reviewing learning

Reviewing is an essential part of learning at any level: individual, team or organization. Reflecting critically on what has been learned, how the learning can be applied and what new learning requirements or opportunities accompany new understanding maintains the pace and quality of learning.

Within the team, however, reviewing of learning plays an additional, vital linking role: it provides the interchange between individual and team mental models. Daniel Kim[28] sees teams as "extended individuals", building on Argyris and Schon's concept of double loop learning, explored earlier. He identifies three situations where team learning is incomplete: situational learning (when learning is not codified for later use); fragmented learning (when the link between individual mental models and shared mental models is broken); and opportunistic learning (when the link is severed between shared mental models and organizational action in order to seize opportunities). By contrast, learning is at its maximum when the process of reviewing/adapting mental models and translating them into action is a smooth continuum between individual, team and organization. What this means in practice is that quality of reflection is vital in the team's ability to conceive of and implement creative change.

Coaching questions for reviewing learning include:

◆ How will we make space and time for reflection on what we have done and not done? (Sometimes called reflection on action.)
◆ How will we ensure that we learn from what we are doing? (Sometimes called reflection in action.)

◆ How do the team mental models help us achieve the task? Do we know what those mental models are and, if not, how will we find out?

Sharing learning

Sharing learning is – or should be – a natural outcome of reflection. The team needs processes to ensure that learning gained by individuals or sub-groups is shared between the rest of the members and, where appropriate, with other teams and/or customers. The process of sharing needs to be both structured – through formal meetings, record keeping and so on – and unstructured – through informal, *ad hoc* encounters and opportunities. Some of the devices for sharing learning include:

◆ Integrating elements of individual learning logs in a team learning log.
◆ Recording questions and answers in a database.

A DATABASE OF FAQS

A small manufacturing company needed to expand its core production teams severalfold two or three times a year to cope with seasonal demand. It took the casual workers a few days to become proficient at the basics, during which time they were a frequent interruption to the permanent employees. As a result, turnover among the permanent employees was relatively high. The simple solution was for each team to create a database of frequently asked questions and appropriate answers. Then, when casual staff had a query, the old hands could simply direct them to this resource. Whenever a query arose that was not covered in the database, a new entry was made. Job satisfaction and retention among the old hands increased substantially.

◆ Holding "show and learn" sessions at team meetings, where everyone is encouraged to present on a specific item of learning they have acquired since the previous meeting.

Coaching questions for sharing learning include:

◆ How will each of us recognize when another team member could benefit from others' experience or knowledge?
◆ What formal or informal coaching and mentoring relationships do we want to establish?

Recognizing and rewarding learning

Finally, having a clear link between effort and recognition for learning reinforces the value placed on the learning process. One of the most frequent barriers to team learning relates to the motivational climate. Spirals of performance are feedback systems. When everything is going well, people and teams feel a high level of self-efficacy. This increase in confidence is highly motivating, so performance continues to climb, in a self-reinforcing spiral. The opposite occurs when things go badly. Perception of self-efficacy drops, and so does performance. Sometimes, the source of the positive or negative spiral can be one element of the team's activity – say a single sale to an important customer, or an industry award for a specific project – that has a knock-on effect on team confidence.

Learning efficiency and quality can be reduced by both positive and negative cycles. Being overconfident – or worse, arrogant – can be a severe barrier to reflection.

Effective learning teams find a variety of ways to demonstrate how valued individual learning and knowledge sharing are, from simple praise at team meetings to more elaborate celebrations around learning milestones. For example, in one team individual learning targets were linked to team-wide rewards. This not only put pressure on individuals to achieve learning goals, but incentivized colleagues to support them in doing so.

Coaching questions for recognizing and rewarding learning include:

- How do we know that useful learning has occurred?
- How would each of us like to be measured and recognized for our contribution to team knowledge?
- How would each of us like to be measured and recognized for putting new knowledge and skills to work?

Building the learning team

Learning teams don't just happen: they need support and guidance from leaders and/or coaches in creating appropriate structures, climate and processes. D'Andrea-O'Brien and Buono[29] identify four key processes involved in building the learning team:

- **Creating a learning culture** requires the leader, if necessary in collusion with the organization, to create reward systems that encourage learning and sharing knowledge. They also build an atmosphere of psychological safety; coach new team members; facilitate "the creation of and commitment to team norms that support inter-member learning; and focus on the quality of member interaction and output". An important part of the last of these items is to articulate and capture a statement of behavioural expectations by which the team operates.
- **Facilitating paradigm shifts** – or in plain language, helping the team make significant transitions in how it thinks and what it does – requires the team to open itself to feedback and information from a much wider range of sources than it might normally do and to be creative both in setting itself new performance challenges and in how it achieves them.

- **Valuing individual and collective strengths** requires processes such as creating an inventory of members' knowledge, skills and abilities.
- Finally, the team needs to develop the **attitudes and communication competence** that allow "the resultant common database of knowledge [to] be added to and manoeuvred in ways that encourage proactive strategic thinking, systems-oriented thinking and creative problem solving". The mechanisms for achieving this include dialogue, discussion, observations and experience sharing. In particular, team members have to recognize that words often mean different things to different people (especially true across cultures) and that they therefore need the "patience, ability and willingness to seek sufficient feedback to ensure that their words – their arguments, recommendations, concerns and so forth – are understood as intended".

International misunderstanding

A practical example is a South African colleague attending meetings of an international steering group in the US. At several successive meetings she expressed her wish to have a subject discussed urgently, saying she would like to "table this", only for the topic to be ignored. Eventually she realized that in American English, she was asking for the issue to be parked for discussion in the future!

Another way of looking at the same issue is as a series of evolutionary stages, in which the team gradually acquires capability and capacity to manage its learning. The goal can be described as team learning maturity, where the team becomes a significant net contributor to organizational learning and an exemplar of good learning practice.

Our learning teams research project identified four levels on the way to team learning maturity:

- **Ad hoc** – no real structure for learning; little understanding among team members of each other's learning needs; no vision of the learning that the team as a whole needs to acquire; few systems to manage learning and knowledge transfer. Access to training may be given as a reward, rather than against a development plan.
- **Externally stimulated** – learning goals and structures are imposed from outside the team. Planned learning consists mainly of sending people on courses, often on request or instruction from a central resource.
- **Internally stimulated** – the team has a clear vision of the learning needed both individually and collectively; everyone has a clear developmental role for themselves and towards other members; there are some basic systems for managing learning within the team.
- **Integrated** – learning goals integrate the needs of the organization, the team and the individual members; people are trained and motivated to fulfil a variety of learning roles towards each other; strong systems for managing learning within the team are supplemented by systems to encourage and manage networking with other teams.

Not surprisingly, we have found relatively few work teams that can honestly say they have reached the integrated level. In all those we have found, one of the key factors is having a leader or manager who has set learning excellence as a priority, spent time planning with the team how to improve its learning systems and practices, and been a role model for coaching, for being coached and for creating opportunities for coaching between members of the team.

How behaviours support the learning team

We found nine recurring behavioural characteristics in our research (see Figure 4.8 overleaf):

FIGURE 4.8

THE NINE KEY BEHAVIOURAL DRIVERS OF A LEARNING TEAM

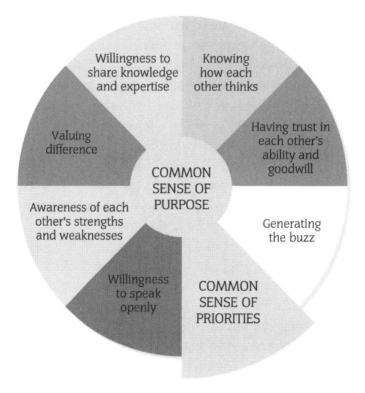

- A **common sense of purpose** is achieved when team members share a clear set of goals. Ideally, these have defined outputs, a link with organizational goals and a shared understanding of what the team as a whole needs to do to achieve the task. Goal clarity informs the team members about what they need to learn and why.
- A **common sense of priorities** follows on from shared goals. Knowing what is important and why enables people to make decisions about what learning needs are most urgent.
- **Willingness to speak openly** is critical to creating genuine dialogue. The longer and more closely a team has worked together, typically the less willing its members are to be constructively

confrontational towards each other. Overcoming this reluctance – giving honest feedback to each other – supports continuous learning.

- **Awareness of each other's strengths and weaknesses** provides a platform for mutual assistance and co-coaching.
- **Valuing difference** establishes the mutual respect that oils the giving and receiving of learning between peers.
- It also helps build **willingness to share knowledge and expertise** – there is no room in the learning team for the concept that "knowledge is power".
- Members of effective learning teams tend rapidly to develop an instinctive **understanding of how each other thinks**. They are able to substitute for each other across a wide range of tasks or decisions.
- In part, this ability derives from **having trust in each other's ability and goodwill** – they have worked at establishing mutual confidence.
- Finally, all the most successful teams in our study – and all the respondents who recalled teams that had been significant learning experiences for them – talked about **generating the buzz**. In fact there are two elements here: buzz is the enjoyment that comes from the social environment, from working with others from whom you can learn. Fizz is the enjoyment that comes from the work itself. When combined, fizz and buzz become powerful motivational vehicles for both learning and task achievement.

The role of the team leader

In our team learning study, we found from the accounts of individuals and teams that team learning was dependent in part or whole on the learning climate and that the team leader was a key factor in creating that climate. Among activities attributed to such team leaders were:

- Encouraging team members to coach and teach each other.
- Encouraging team members to participate in other types of team, so that they brought back new knowledge.
- Sharing their own learning needs with the team.
- Actively managing the balance between task activity and learning activity.

How ready is your team for learning?

It seems that the effectiveness of learning within teams depends on a number of factors, including the level of psychological safety, the role adopted by the team leader, the existence and use of processes to manage learning and the level of diversity within the team. The differences in team dynamics also influence the learning approaches that a team coach can initiate. In the next chapter, we explore some of the common issues that team coaches face and how to manage them.

FINAL COACHING QUESTION

How mature and/or competent is this team in its approach to learning?

CHAPTER FIVE

Managing team coaching

"If coaching individuals has its difficulties and complexities, then these are multiplied when coaching teams." |
Myles Downey, *Effective Coaching*[1]

This chapter has no core theme, but it does have a core rationale. The effective team coach needs to be able to respond appropriately and often without much time for preparation to a whole range of issues. This is not an easy role for someone who has trouble thinking on their feet.

The areas I have selected as being of particular value and importance fall into three broad categories: managing interpersonal dynamics, temporal issues and managing key processes.

Managing interpersonal dynamics is about helping the team develop the internal capability to surface and deal with conflict, to build collective emotional intelligence and collective self-belief, to manage stress, and to establish and maintain a healthy coaching climate.

Temporal issues relate to decisions about when and how the coach should intervene, to the nature of the team's temporal orientation (how it thinks about past, present and future and the appropriateness of this orientation to the team's task), and to time management.

Managing key processes is about goal setting, understanding how the team functions, and building its capacity in terms of creativity, systems thinking and communication. It also covers evaluating the impact of coaching.

Why did I select these particular themes? Partly because they are all (with the exception of managing conflict and setting goals) poorly covered in the existing practitioner literature on team coaching. And partly, too, because these are all issues that have forced me or colleagues to step back and reflect on our own practice. So no apologies, this is a pot-pourri of aspects that it is helpful for the team coach to be aware of and be prepared to deal with, as and if they arise.

Managing interpersonal dynamics

Although team members don't have to *like* each other for the team to function well, there is a minimal level of rapport, mutual respect and understanding required to sustain the communication needed for consistent high performance. To paraphrase the words of the survivor of a team of two highly successful comic scriptwriters, who worked together for more than three decades:

> "He was, in many respects, completely untrustworthy and often very frustrating. He was also a genius. I decided early on that I had to supply the morals in our partnership and somehow it worked – brilliantly."

In this partnership – as in so many successful marriages – the grit in the oyster was a constant driver of performance.

In all relationships, there is a choice between trying to change behaviours, and learning to live with and take advantage of them while ameliorating their worst effects. Neither tactic is likely to work without a reasonably clear understanding of the relationship dynamics. A critical task for the team coach, therefore, is to help the team become sufficiently comfortable about dealing with emotions that it can engage in the kind of open dialogue that produces insights into behavioural interactions: what drives them, what impact they have on each of the parties involved and how appropriately they are managed. It is important to recognize that everyone has a lower capacity to cope with some emotions than with others. Acknowledging both one's own and colleagues' capacity in this respect is a valuable first step in creating the appreciative and supportive environment in which coaching can flourish and remarkable deeds be performed by the team.

All too often, however, the team coach is called in when relationships have hit what more senior managers consider to be a nadir (but is often actually a small plateau on a steep downward slope!). So we deal first with the issue of surfacing and managing conflict within the team.

Helping the team manage conflict

Conflict, as we saw in Chapter 2, comes in three types – relationship, task and process – and only the latter two have the potential to be positive. The challenge for the team coach is to minimize negative conflict while maximizing positive conflict.

It helps to further categorize the nature of intra-team conflict in terms of the urgency of the situation and who is directly involved. Broadly speaking, there are three levels of urgency: immediate (a crisis that has a direct and current effect on performance of one or both parties, or the team as a whole); short term (needs to be resolved, but is best dealt with in a planned dialogue); and long term (the development of skills within the team to foresee and manage potential conflict without the need for coaching intervention). In addition, conflict can be categorized by the number and influence of its immediate protagonists (or antagonists, to be more precise). Conflict may occur between individuals, between groups within the team, across the team as a whole, or between the team and other teams. In each case, the coach will need to adopt a subtly different approach.

In the context of an immediate need to resolve or ameliorate a conflict, the initial goal for the coach must be to get both sides to retreat from the high ground and reflect. In any conflict, there are usually three parties: me/us, him/her/them and it. "It" is the

FIGURE 5.1

FAULT-FREE CONFLICT MANAGEMENT

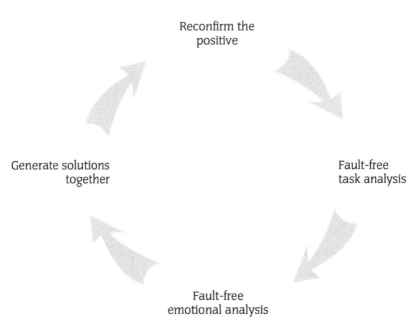

Reconfirm the
positive

Generate solutions
together

Fault-free
task analysis

Fault-free
emotional analysis

negative interpretation of each other's actions and motives, along with the stresses that obscure our normal ability to be rational about them. "It" is the unseen partner, the evil genius (EG for short) who escalates conflict. Especially in the case of conflict between individuals, the coach acts to remind those involved of the common goal, steer them towards a short period of reflection (cooling off is not enough – there has to be a specific, beneficial question for them to think through), and focus them individually on identifying and taking partial responsibility for the EG.

The coach may help one or both parties individually to describe the EG. If both have done so, it becomes possible to have a more reasoned discussion, with the parties focusing on achieving an accommodation that will benefit themselves a well as the team as a whole.

Another practical technique that the coach can apply in this meeting is **fault-free conflict management** (see Figure 5.1). Here the coach initially allows the participants to make only positive statements and to reconfirm that there is mutual respect and mutual value in the relationship – even if it is currently a bit strained! In the second phase of the dialogue only task issues can be discussed and the rule is no blame. The coach encourages each coachee to work through openly and in sequence:

◆   What I'm trying to achieve and why.
◆   What I'm having difficulty doing (but not whose fault it is).
◆   What problems are resulting for the customers, the rest of the team or other stakeholders.

Next, the coach, who has so far encouraged everyone to put aside their emotional baggage, asks them to reveal:

◆   How I want to feel.
◆   How I actually feel.
◆   What is making me feel the way I do (being as open as possible about the range of causes: internal, stemming from the relationship in question, external to the relationship).

Finally, the coach asks each coachee for a solution to part of the other person's problem, encouraging them to be generous in offering changes in what they do. This coaching conversation is not all about the EG, but its broad focus on the EG enables participants to work round their egos and contain their emotional overload.

Conflict source analysis

In working with conflict that needs to be resolved in the short term but not immediately, the coach can take a more detailed, analytical approach, helping the team to work through the elements in Table 5.1 overleaf. Each element provides an opportunity to develop shared understanding from three perspectives as appropriate: individual, groups within the team and the team as a whole.

TABLE 5.1

UNDERSTANDING THE COMPONENTS OF CONFLICT WITHIN THE TEAM

CONFLICT TYPE	GOALS • INDIVIDUAL • GROUP • TEAM	MOTIVATIONS • INDIVIDUAL • GROUP • TEAM	VALUES • INDIVIDUAL • GROUP • TEAM	METHODS • INDIVIDUAL • GROUP • TEAM
Relationship conflict				
Task conflict				
Process conflict				

Goals relate to what each stakeholder sees the team being there for. Good questions include:

◆   What do we want to achieve and why?
◆   What is the benefit of what we are trying to do?
◆   What are we trying *not* to do?
◆   Whose goal is it? (Who owns the goal?)

Motivations relate to the intrinsic rewards that individuals, sub-groups and the team as a whole expect to get both from achieving the goal and *from the process of doing so*. In a sports context, the latter could be described as the pleasure of playing as differentiated from the pleasure of winning.

Values concern the rules and principles that underpin our approaches to the task and to other people: how we make and act on judgements. What is important to us at an individual level may not be important at a team level and vice versa.

Finally, **methods** describe the processes by which we attempt to achieve the various levels of goals. A preference for a particular method might be the result of habit ("We've always done it this way and it works, so why change it?"); personality ("I can't see the point in going into this amount of detail"); or a rational reaction to external change.

Mapping the potential components of conflict in this way builds a shared understanding of the diversity of perspective and experience in the team. With effective coaching, it helps people gain greater respect for this diversity. It also reveals where goals, motivations, values and methods may be in conflict with each other.

Occasionally, conflict may pitch one individual against the rest of the team for "letting the side down". This can be highly destructive to relationships all round, because members learn to fear what will happen if they in turn make a serious mistake. Ineffective line managers sometimes choose individuals to be scapegoats for the team's failures and overtly or covertly encourage other team members to follow their lead. (We call it the Jonah syndrome.) Not only does this prevent team members innovating or challenging, but it leads to a recurrent cycle where newcomers are in favour to begin with, then are gradually sidelined as they are revealed to be less perfect than the manager has mentally built them up to be.

Helping a manager with the Jonah syndrome may sometimes require a depth of psychotherapeutic competence beyond that of coaches from non-therapeutic disciplines. Deep-seated narcissism and psychopathy are unlikely to be resolved by a coaching conversation on its own. In most other cases, where the team appears to "gang up" on one or two individuals, the coach can help reduce conflict by ensuring that everyone is aware of the spectrum of personality types in the team and the impact of these differences. The following story illustrates the point.

NOT A BLOCK AFTER ALL

Alex was constantly finding himself the odd one out in the sales development team of a large retailer. He had begun his career in accounts in a business-to-business setting, but had overcome stereotypes to switch to sales after two years and had been highly successful. Customers liked his measured, patient style and his ability to help them work out exactly what they wanted, on what were long-term, high-cost purchases. When he joined the retailer, it was with a reputation as someone who had driven sales growth relentlessly. After a few months in his new team, however, he gained a very different reputation. Alex was "the blocker", the person who always pointed out the downsides to proposed innovations. Eventually, his boss brought in a coach to "sort him out".

After the first session, the coach recognized that this was a team issue, not a problem with one individual. She persuaded the boss to allow her to assess the team role profiles of all the members and to arrange a joint discussion of the results. As she had expected, Alex was the only person in the team with strong preferences for structure and for standards. When the team shared their profiles, they were surprised that Alex was as motivated as they were towards getting things done. From the ensuing discussion, it emerged that the reason Alex kept trying to apply the brakes was that he believed the team didn't really understand what the customers wanted now, or would want in the next two years. There were too many unproven assumptions.

Alex was able to present some evidence from *ad hoc* research he had done with one of the medium-sized customers. Other team members dismissed this with the comment, "They always want the moon!" The coach then asked how they distinguished between positively and negatively demanding customers. It wasn't a distinction they had made before, but the manager eventually interposed to point out that, whatever Alex's customer demanded now, customers in general demanded one or two years later. The meeting ended with an agreement that Alex should carry out some detailed and structured market research.

When Alex presented his report, it proposed far more radical change than his colleagues had envisaged when they complained about him being a blocker. It required a higher investment than had been budgeted for, but promised substantially faster sales growth. The coach was asked to assist again, this time to help the team examine its commitment to real change and to develop the tactics for selling the increased investment to top management. By focusing on task/process conflict, the coach helped the team resolve the relationship conflict, to the benefit of all concerned.

In the longer term, a coach can help the team develop the skills of dialogue, which will help members resolve conflict without coaching intervention. The more effectively and transparently the coach explains the process by which they address conflict, the easier it will be for the team members to adopt the same behaviours and tools when needed.

Raising the emotional intelligence of the team

The ability of the team to deliver the kind of behaviours essential to managing task achievement and continuous learning is heavily dependent on their individual and joint **emotional intelligence**. The idea of a team having emotional intelligence (EQ) may sound strange, but it is very real. The collective emotional response to stimuli tends to be habitual and often unconscious. Equally, the more emotionally aware the team is, the more capable it should be of managing conflict.

The team coach has two tasks in this context: raising individual and collective EQ, and engaging the team members in helping improve each other's EQ.

City Homes is the housing department for Cambridge City
Council in the UK. It is responsible for 8,200 properties in the
city and employs 1,143 staff, of whom 150 are employed in
housing management. The top team is composed of a chief
executive and several housing officers. Coach Margaret
Chapman was tasked with helping the team increase its overall emotional intelligence, so that it was better equipped to
cope with a series of organizational challenges.

The coaching intervention consisted of several elements. First,
the coach interviewed all the team members to draw up a
needs analysis of the outcomes expected from improving the
overall team EQ. The goals identified from these interviews
included developing a greater sense of team cohesion, identity
and purpose; building working relationships both within the
team and with a range of stakeholders; improving openness,
trust, supportiveness and shared learning; and creating a
more dynamic, achievement-oriented working environment.

Then all the team members completed a self-scoring
emotional intelligence diagnostic, the Boston Emotional
Intelligence Questionnaire, which consists of 44 statements
relating to emotion-focused actions. The results were
discussed in detail at a series of five team coaching workshops. The leader's EQ was assessed using a different, 360-
degree instrument.

Two further elements rounded off the coaching intervention:
one-to-one coaching sessions after each workshop, and a "feeling diary" in which team members recorded their emotions
over the intervening periods. These were both aimed at supporting participants through the inevitable lapses of behaviour,
building their ability to anticipate and manage setbacks.

In addition, the coach helped the team evaluate the changes
that had taken place. When the diagnostic was repeated, it

showed a substantial increase in self-perception of emotional intelligence on four of the five EQ factors (self-awareness, emotion management, self-motivation and relationship management, but not emotional coaching) for all team members except the leader. The rest of the team had an increased estimation of the team leader's EQ.

Feedback from the participants strongly supported the view that one-to-one and team coaching were both important and complementary. The group sessions allowed the team to establish solutions and ways of working together; they also made the process as a whole feel much less like therapy.

The outcomes of the team coaching programme were perceived increases in team cohesion, collaborative behaviours and awareness/understanding/valuing of individual differences, both within the team and in relation to other teams.

The intelligence of the team (its IQ) is its ability to use logic, rational deduction and effective decision-making processes in pursuit of its goals. Most teams and individuals think of themselves as rational beings, but we typically make decisions on a mixture of values and logic. A key task for the team coach is often to help people develop the skills to enhance the awareness of emotional influences on decision making, while at the same time improving the reasoning processes that the team employs.

Received wisdom says that you can't normally improve the innate IQ of an adult individual. Whether that applies to a team as a whole is debatable. But you can recognize and employ people's different strengths in the nine intelligences identified by Gardner,[2] including IQ, according to the situation; and you can help individuals and the team develop **coping processes** that provide a systematic approach to managing the decision-making tasks.

On emotional intelligence specifically, the coach can use any of several self-diagnostic or 360-degree questionnaires (the latter clearly give a more rounded and hence more useful perspective) to provide the data for this kind of conversation. Members of teams who share a language for talking about emotions tend, at least anecdotally, to be much more competent in confronting dysfunctional behaviour, offering and asking for support and accommodating each other's emotional weaknesses. They also tend to be more aware that weaknesses are often strengths taken to excess or misapplied, and they are more likely to value the underlying strengths.

It is this integrated understanding and application of emotional intelligence at an individual level that creates the conditions for collective EQ, which we can define as the team's ability to manage emotions in a manner that supports the team task. Measuring collective EQ is difficult, but coaching dialogue can at least pose the questions against which broad assessments can be made. Some of these questions are:

- Do we frequently regret our initial emotional response to an externally generated issue?
- Are we broadly aware of how our team colleagues feel about issues?
- Are we able to talk openly within the team about our feelings?
- Are we able to manage intra-team conflict confidently and positively?
- Do we respect and value differences in personality and perspective?
- Are we making effective use of each other's emotional strengths?
- Do we recognize instinctively when a colleague is in need of support?
- Does every member feel emotionally supported when they need it?
- Do we have a collective view about what we care about and why?
- Do we have a reputation for being understanding towards people outside the team?
- Do we have a high level of emotional resilience (i.e. the capacity to bounce back when things go wrong)?

Developing collective self-belief

Myles Downey,[3] exploring coaching in the team context, points out that just as for individuals

> "the single greatest factor that inhibits performance is self-doubt… in a group situation, doubt is contagious. And as it grips, it deepens, ultimately, into panic. In a team 'interference' is multiplied… and, in the worst cases, performance diminishes to the point that one person could do the work of the team in a fraction of the time."

It is very common for coaches to be assigned "problem" teams to work with. The very fact that the team is seen externally as a problem usually ensures that its members will have a reduced belief in their ability to deliver what is asked of them. The techniques of solutions-focused coaching have a role to play here, but so too does the broader approach of reassessing assumptions.

One method that seems to work well in many situations is to examine a range of assumptions, starting at any point on the list below:

- Assumptions about me, my values, my ability and what I want
- Assumptions about the team, our values, our collective capability and what we want
- Assumptions about the constraints we work under (are they really constraints or opportunities to demonstrate creativity?)
- Assumptions about the nature of success and failure
- Assumptions about what we could achieve

The sequence of coaching questions runs something like this:

- What assumptions are you making about this issue?
- What is your basis for these assumptions?
- How do you know that this basis is accurate?

◆ How useful is the assumption? What need does it fulfil?

◆ What would be a more useful assumption?

◆ What stops you adopting that new assumption?

◆ What can you do now that would help you switch to the new assumption?

◆ What could others do to help? How could you get them to do so?

◆ Why are we still talking about this? (Time for action!)

Managing stress within the team

As long ago as 1908, two Harvard researchers, Robert Yerkes and John Dodson, devised the Yerkes–Dodson law, which defines the relationship between stress and performance. They found that a certain amount of initial stress is positive. Our blood pressure and heart rate increase; we become more alert, more focused, more efficient. But sustained stress or stress above this alertness-raising level leads to rapidly declining levels of performance (see Figure 5.2). This applies in all stress situations, for example taking an exam, making a presentation or competing in a sports event.

Herbert Benson, an associate professor of medicine at Harvard Medical School, has researched hundreds of teams looking at how they innovate. He finds that there is a common pattern of events that can be replicated. It seems that the mind is at its most creative when it has been taken to the top of the stress curve, where it is most alert, then rapidly relaxed into a state of wellbeing. An increase in nitric oxide release in the brain creates what he calls "calm commotion" and increases activity "in areas of the brain associated with attention, space–time concepts and decision making... subjects who learn to do this as a matter of course perform at consistently higher levels."[4]

Benson describes this process as a breakout sequence, which takes place in four steps:

FIGURE 5.2

THE YERKES–DODSON LAW

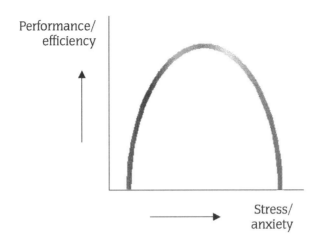

1. Struggle with a thorny problem. Worry at it until you feel unproductive and stressed, or bored.
2. Walk away from it and do something completely different and relaxing – exercise, complete a sudoku or simply take a nap.
3. Insight occurs involuntarily as the mind re-engages with the issue or task.
4. Returning to normal, the sense of wellbeing continues but both the stress and the relaxation stimuli have subsided.

The coach working with a team can create the conditions for Step 1 ahead of a workshop or meeting by asking people to think deeply before they arrive about a difficult problem and how they and their job relate to it. Ramping up the stress levels by establishing the downsides of not tackling the problem and the complexities of getting to grips with it may help. Then the team should have at least 10 minutes of relaxation, before re-engaging with the issue. This makes effective use of the body's natural creativity rhythms.

Creating the climate for team coaching

A fundamental issue in creating the climate is to enable the issues that affect team performance to surface. It often takes a long time and a great deal of trust building to get to the point where this happens easily. The coach can speed up the process by asking everyone, over the course of several days or a week, to list all the unresolved issues that create background noise in their mind, both work related and non-work. Giving examples helps: "I need to sort out my library of PowerPoint™ slides." "I have to build a better working relationship with the accounts department." "I know there is something wrong with this process, but I can't work out what it is." Each member of the team is invited to:

- Reveal how many such issues they have listed, providing an opportunity to discuss the impact and possible shared solutions to issues overload.
- "Post" individual issues openly within the team, to determine who else shares the problem and therefore has an interest in tackling it.
- Offer to act as coach to a colleague on specific issues.

There is no compulsion to reveal the whole of one's list and, indeed, it is better that everyone posts only a limited number of the most nagging issues. The process can be repeated from time to time. A useful variation after several sessions is to ask everyone to post at least one issue that has remained continually on their list but not been prioritized. (These issues can sometimes be the most cathartic of all when they are finally addressed through coaching.)

Other factors in creating a climate conducive to team coaching include psychological safety (explored in Chapter 3) and developing the ability of team members to coach and be coached. Unless the coach is also the team leader or manager, it is difficult to create psychological safety. Even then, it takes time, patience and consistent positive role modelling on the part of the leader, for example by being genuinely open about their feelings and their needs for learning from the team. For the external coach, it may be necessary to spend some months working with the team leader, helping them build the expectation of mutual openness within the team, before considering embarking on a team coaching endeavour.

The range of excuses for not coaching and for not seeking coaching is vast, but they boil down in most cases to fear of discomfort or embarrassment and/or lack of confidence in one's own ability to manage the coaching process. So it can greatly help the team coaching process if all the participants have been through some form of skills training before team coaching begins.

TEAM COACHING WORKSHOPS IN A SPANISH MANUFACTURER

In 1990, a Spanish subsidiary of a multinational industrial company reorganized the manufacturing structure of two of its factories, reducing the number of management layers and organizing the workforce into teams. Every team leader led three or four teams with 20 members in each, and was responsible for managing the team's quality, costs, time and human resources. The team was supported through centralized training programmes and the normal non-assembly functions: quality, logistics, maintenance and engineering. In 1999, further restructuring delegated much greater responsibility than before to the team leaders.

In 2001, a development programme began aimed at improving productivity and teamwork. This involved top management and also the team leaders who reported to them. The team leaders received a range of management training; directors and managers were trained in coaching, which the company defines as "a management practice focused on the person and on personal performance". Directors received 360-degree feedback as part of the development of their self-awareness. By 2005, all had been trained, most had experience in one-to-one coaching and two pilot sets of six team leaders had been exposed to a team experience.

Before joining the team coaching workshops, these team leaders had received a programme of coaching for three months. The workshops were designed to help them reflect on their coaching practice and for them to help each other develop greater coaching competence. Explains external coach/consultant Manuela Uría:

"Every person shared with the group a practice of coaching and told us about the objectives they wanted to achieve. The group listened and helped the person with questions, doubts and assumptions, with the objective of widening the focus of their thinking. At the end of the six sessions, they evaluated the learning, the obstacles (such as time) and their achievements. They found it particularly useful to have a space with colleagues and two coaches where they could feel free to share their day-to-day problems with colleagues, away from the urgency of their normal work. They also valued the way the coaches/facilitators/mentors helped them in opening new perspectives, or taking into account other issues, or reflecting on their own emotions."

Among the learning from the workshops:

- The need to set aside sufficient time for real reflection. The follow-on team coaching sets now meet for two-and-a-half hours every workshop.

- Although the managers are used to setting objectives for the production system, doing the same in a personal context is a big challenge.

- It may be better for the team to be made up of volunteers, rather than people chosen by the senior managers. People whose management style is very directive do not fit in well. They may find excuses not to join in, and their attention may be elsewhere, on other priorities.

◈   There needs to be a clear link between the manager's current work objectives and their personal development plan.

◈   Coaching by peers helps to focus the practice of coaching: it provides different visions, widening the mental map of the manager and enriching their perspectives.

◈   The coaching environment made it safe to talk openly about difficulties that managers had with colleagues in their teams and to view the problems from a distance.

◈   Confidentiality is as essential in the process of team coaching as it is in one-to-one coaching.

Written by Manuela Uría, an external coach/consultant at Adhominem BPI Group, based in Spain. Her email address is: manuelauria@hotmail.com.

Temporal issues

In Chapter 3 we examined the research around when team coaching interventions are likely to be most effective. Whichever team type the coach is working with, the wrong intervention at the wrong time can cause substantial disruption to team cohesion and performance. Equally, establishing with the team an expectation of the kind of learning dialogue that will be helpful to them at key points is likely to improve cohesion and performance.

Just-in-time team coaching

Kolb's learning cycle[5] – concrete experience, reflective observation, abstract conceptualization, active experimentation – provides a useful starting point for evaluating the team task against the need for different styles of learning conversation. The key questions are:

- At what times in the work cycle will we find it most helpful to observe, to theorize/analyse, to plan, and just to get on and do?
- What questions should we be asking ourselves at each of these points?

Whatever team type and whatever stage of evolution the team has reached, these questions establish an expectation of dialogue based on the realities of the work at the time. Overlaying these questions with what we now know about a team's receptivity to different types of coaching intervention at the beginning, mid point and near the end of a task cycle generates further coaching questions, such as:

- When do we want to focus on roles and responsibilities? On processes and systems? On strategy? On capturing learning?
- When will it be most helpful to review relationships within the team? Relationships with people outside the team?

In practice, of course, no matter how well planned the sequence of coaching themes and styles is, in the real world issues come up that demand rapid resolution and cannot wait until the most auspicious time to be addressed. Rather than just launch into such issues-based coaching, however, the team coach should already have agreed with the team the process for these *ad hoc* sessions (and the budget, if they are an external coach!). Process questions include:

- When do we need the whole team to attend the coaching session and when will fewer than that be acceptable?
- If not everyone is involved, how will we make sure that those not included are brought up to speed and can take some ownership of any decisions reached?
- What is the minimum level of preparation by the team that is acceptable in making the coaching process work?
- Is this best as one detailed team coaching session or a short session to work out what we want and what we do and don't

know, followed by a longer session once we have more substantial data to work with?

- How will we build in sufficient time and space for calm reflection when people are in crisis action mode?
- Is this really a coaching session or a crisis meeting using some coaching techniques?
- Is there any difference in the outcomes expected between these short-notice coaching sessions and the planned sessions?

The probability is high that the answers to each of these questions will only become clear as the occasion arises. However, thinking the broad issues through with the team ahead of time means that less precious time will need to be spent on process issues, leaving more to devote to the coaching dialogue itself.

Temporal orientation

People differ considerably in their temporal orientation. Cross-cultural comparisons, for example, show wide variations in how people think about time; these are reflected in both language and behaviour. The sharp division in western thinking between past, present and future is not reflected in all cultures.

Within the Anglo-Saxon culture, however, it is generally the case that people tend to have a preference to position issues in the past, the present or the future. People who have a **past** orientation tend to prefer routine and what is known. They take as their reference point what has happened before, rather than what is happening now or may happen in the future. They are often good at establishing historical analogies, which can be very helpful, for example, in avoiding repeating past mistakes. However, they may also tend to miss current and future opportunities, and to be reluctant either to experiment or to question the present validity of solutions and processes that used to work.

People with a predominantly **present** orientation, at the extreme, live for the moment. They take the view that "what is done, is done" and are eager to move on to the next problem or opportunity. While this is highly beneficial in terms of achievement, they tend to miss opportunities to reflect on and learn from experience. They may, for example, be always busy but not necessarily delivering the goods or improving performance.

People with a strong **future** orientation are either visionaries (when effective) or dreamers (when not effective). They may lack the sense of urgency inherent in present-oriented colleagues, but they are often very good at working steadily towards a long-term goal, using what happens in the present to create conditions under which that goal may come about.

In practice, both managers and the organizations in which they work need to have a balance between all three temporal orientations. The advantages of a strong orientation in one can very easily be undermined by a lack of attention or lack of capability in the others. The team coach or mentor can help in the following ways:

◆ Raise awareness of what the team's dominant temporal orientation is.
◆ Examine the implications of the temporal orientation.
◆ Capitalize on individual variations in temporal orientation between team members.
◆ Develop with the team tools and processes to ensure that it achieves the balance of temporal orientation that will most effectively help it meet its goals.

Time management

Time management is one of the most common issues that an executive coach encounters in dealing with individuals. But many of the same principles apply directly to how the team uses its finite resources of time and mental energy. It's not practical or reasonable to expect the team to work at full throttle all the time: variation in pace is important in maintaining interest and concentration. It's rather like working muscles. Athletes learn to pace exercise so that heavy exertion is followed by a period of lighter activity that breaks down and disperses the by-products of muscle use that cause cramp. Similarly, teams need to intersperse concentrated effort with periods of light-heartedness; action with reflection; doing with reviewing. A high-performing team and its members develop a rhythm of work that builds what we might call performance stamina.

One of the most interesting recent analyses of the psychology of inefficient use of time by individuals is by Steven Berglas,[6] who has also researched extensively into the psychology of coaching. He identifies four principal varieties of "time abusers", whose individual time management foibles may undermine team performance. Each of these characteristic styles of ineffective time management may also describe how a team as a whole functions. The four styles are:

◆ **Pre-emptives** – "people who compulsively beat the clock. They finish a project weeks ahead of schedule and always seem to be in control." What's wrong with that? Berglas explains that they make very poor team players, being focused on their own obsession with avoiding criticism. Because they have always moved on to the next project, they are often not available to others who need their input at later stages of the original project. They create a kind of temporal dislocation between their work and that of others.

FLY TIPPING

I have seen a similar dislocation in a marketing team (where the manager actually had a sign in his office saying "If it's worth doing, it's worth doing now") that would race to complete and launch new campaigns, on the basis that there was always a tight window of market opportunity. Relationships with the regional sales teams were poor, however, because it took time to educate the salespeople and for them to reach the bulk of customers. One sales manager described the marketing department's practice as "fly tipping".

- **People-pleasers** – people who take on more and more responsibility out of fear of authority, with the result that they commit too much of their time to unproductive projects and are routinely late with the projects that matter.

PERMISSION TO SAY NO

The HR department of a large utility illustrates the same phenomenon at a team level. The occasion was a workshop to examine why HR had such a poor reputation within the company, when everyone was working so hard to deliver what they were tasked with. One of the senior members of the team had just returned from "stress leave" and two others had recently resigned because they felt the organization did not support them. The insight breakthrough came when they analysed what was important for the organization and compared it to what they were asked and expected to spend their time on. There wasn't much correlation between the two. The outcome was a strategy to confront top management with a detailed description of where the department could add most value, with a strong supporting business case for each point, and to ask top management for permission to say no to other activities.

- **Perfectionists** – people "who take more time than allotted to satisfy deeply internalized standards of excellence". Like pre-emptives, they tend to be isolationists. Their obsession with detail tends to irritate colleagues greatly.

A team example here is the new product development team that created a military radio that would work in all climates. By the time the product was ready for market, after exhaustive testing from the Arctic to the jungles of the Equator, a new wave of technology was in the wings that made this relatively heavy piece of equipment obsolete. Customers opted to wait a year for the new product and the company's investment was largely wasted.

◆ **Procrastinators** – people who find all manner of excuses for not focusing on the task. Berglas identifies the roots of this compulsive non-delivery in a combination of overly high self-expectations and fear of failure.

DELIVERING ON PROMISES

A team in a publishing company had a remarkable track record of contributing to programmes and initiatives across the sector. It also entered an annual business game contest, in which it always performed well and won on one occasion. Yet other teams were frustrated by its apparent inability to deliver on promises internally. The more internal peers complained, the more the team sought reaffirmation and praise externally. Eventually almost the whole team was fired.

Like all stereotypes, there is a little of several of these characters in each of us and in most teams. By asking the question "How well do we use our available time and energy?" the team coach stimulates reflection on what is arguably one of the most important influencers of team performance. One simple approach to answering the question is to determine:

◆ The amount of time and mental energy the team has available on a weekly, monthly or annual basis.

- How much time can reasonably be allocated to high-concentration work, to low-concentration but necessary work and to reflection/review/learning (taking into account the need for natural rhythms of high and low mental energy).
- What critical tasks does the team have to deliver?
- What time and mental energy are needed to do these to the quality level required (bearing in mind the innate tendency to underestimate the effort involved).
- What time and mental energy are left over for other activities and less important tasks?
- How does this compare with what we actually do?
- To what extent would key stakeholders outside the team agree with this analysis?

If there is a big difference between the ideal and actual use of time and mental energy, there is a need to investigate more deeply and to recognize that some form of time abuse is probably occurring.

Further coaching questions include:

- To what extent is the time abuse internally or externally generated?
- What do we want collectively to do about it?

Managing key processes

It was, I believe, the late, great Peter Drucker who opined that every system created by man eventually ends up delivering the opposite result to that intended. He was thinking, in particular, of governmental processes, but the principle seems to apply universally. Unless systems are truly dynamic, constantly adapting to the environment in which they operate, they gradually become less and less able to deliver what was intended. For a team, understanding how its key processes – technological, administrative and interpersonal –

work both in principle and in fact is a key part of collective performance management. In this section we examine some of the issues relating to understanding and managing critical team processes, starting with perhaps the most important, in terms of effectiveness: achieving goal clarity.

Achieving goal clarity

We've discussed this topic from several angles already, so here's a simple way of achieving a clearer goal focus. Every team, whatever its dynamics, needs a simple method of testing decisions and task approaches against its priority goals. A touchstone question is one that provides a quick check, either for individuals working away from the team or for the team as a whole. The classic corporate touchstone question was that from Clarks, a British shoemaker: "Does it sell shoes?" Clarks attributed much of its success and survival to this simple test of determining where to spend its resources. The equivalent for a specific team might be "Will this keep us in business for the next 10 years?" or "Will this give us 100% customer satisfaction?"

Simple as the touchstone question is, generating it and using it effectively usually require considerable reflection and disciplined thinking. The starting point is a discussion around what the team is there for. The coach can help this thinking process by asking team members to take the perspective of a variety of stakeholders, including themselves, to both what the team's priority role should be and what it should not be. Is it possible to find a touchstone question that encompasses all these perspectives? If team members can, is the question sufficiently sharp to be of real value in making decisions? If the question is not sufficiently sharp, can they develop a different one that is?

What does the team actually do?

For the team to achieve both clarity of goal and clarity of process, the coach may need to stimulate dialogue at a number of levels. One of the simplest levels is represented in Figure 5.3 (which you may remember from Chapter 2). The team needs to distinguish between the tasks it has to carry out to achieve the goals and what it needs to do to make those tasks practical and effective. The latter includes activities such as team building and planning. At the same time, there is a distinction in the minds of team members between tasks and processes related to the internal and the external environments.[7]

FIGURE 5.3

ACTIVITY DIAGNOSIS AT THE SIMPLEST LEVEL

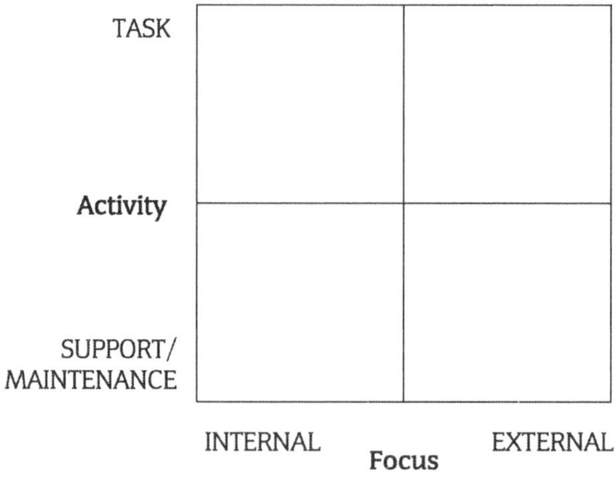

Considering these issues separately enables the team to analyse what effort it needs to put into each quadrant, what priorities it wishes to adopt and what strategies it should apply in managing these complementary activities.

Analysing the team functioning

One of the simplest ways to help the team understand its own workings is to conduct a detailed discussion and review based around three team foci: task, learning and behaviour. Under each heading, the coach helps the team define what needs to happen and what does happen against three sub-foci: roles, processes and capabilities.

In this context, **roles** are what people have to do to achieve the intended shared outcome. Sometimes roles can usefully be categorized in terms of psychological profile and behavioural preference, as in the various team role inventories commonly used to audit team composition. At other times, they may best be derived from the task, learning or behaviour focus itself and will therefore be specific rather than generic. Or a team may benefit from seeing itself from both perspectives.

Processes relate to how the team achieves the task, learning or behavioural goal. Drawing up a process map, identifying how each sub-activity links with others to produce the intended final outcome and where the potential failure points lie, is a standard approach for addressing quality issues.

Capabilities relate to the resources the team holds (or needs) to achieve the goal: knowledge, funds, equipment and so on.

Useful questions for exploring roles include:

◆ What won't get done if no one takes responsibility for it?
◆ What questions do we need to ask ourselves frequently, and how?
◆ What do we individually and collectively tend to avoid doing/procrastinate over?
◆ From what different perspectives should we examine issues relating to this team focus?
◆ Is there enough difference of perspectives to stimulate healthy dialogue around how we do things?
◆ How consistent are we in managing the processes of strategic thinking, decision making, reviewing and reflecting?
◆ How effective are we in these? Where we are ineffective, what roles could some or all of us play in addressing the issue?
◆ What are the critical ways in which we and our colleagues contribute to each team focus, both in terms of what we do and

how we do it? In what ways does each of us sometimes detract from each of the team foci?

◆ What roles are suggested by our level of task interdependence?

Useful questions for exploring processes include:

◆ How do we know this is the best way to do this?
◆ What would happen if we did some or all of the key elements in exactly the opposite way?
◆ Where are the points where things are most likely to go wrong? Which are most damaging if they do go wrong?
◆ Where are the points that we earn most "brownie points"?
◆ What bits of the process do we like most/least? (This can also provide clues about roles.)
◆ Do we review processes sufficiently frequently/in sufficient depth?
◆ What other businesses/activities can we benchmark our processes against?
◆ Are our processes appropriate for the balance we need between interdependence and autonomy?
◆ Which bits of the process do we least/best understand?

Useful questions for exploring capability include:

◆ What do resource restraints prevent us doing? To what extent does that matter?
◆ Do we have the right skills and experience mix for our current task and learning foci?
◆ What external resources can we call on? How effective are we at identifying and accessing these resources?
◆ How well do we use the capability we have? (For example are people over-qualified for their jobs and, if so, what are the implications of that?)
◆ Is our capability growing?

Similarly at the level of the three foci, useful questions about task focus include:

◆   What are we trying to achieve *as a team*?
◆   How clear are we about that goal?
◆   How will that help achieve the broader organizational or societal goals?
◆   How committed are we?
◆   How will we know when we are on target?

Useful questions about the learning focus include:

◆   What knowledge and skills are important for fulfilling the team task (now and in the medium term)?
◆   What is our plan for achieving that learning?
◆   How will we know when we have got there?
◆   What are our individual and collective responsibilities for learning?

Useful questions for exploring behaviour include:

◆   What does each of us do that supports our colleagues in their roles and activities?
◆   What does each of us do that makes it more difficult for our colleagues to carry out their roles and activities?
◆   What issues/behaviours do we feel most uncomfortable about owning up to in relation to ourselves and to our colleagues?
◆   What behaviours would make us more effective as a team?
◆   What do we fear most? Desire most?
◆   What makes us feel really good/less good working with our colleagues?
◆   What should we do more of/less of both individually and collectively?
◆   How can we stimulate the positive expression of each behavioural preference and personality and minimize the negative?
◆   What behaviours would best support our various roles in the team?

Raising the creativity of the team

CREATIVE ACCOUNTING

It had to be the accounts department. After all, what use is a stereotype if people don't live up to it? "We're not paid to be creative," said the manager.

"Are you paid to be helpful?"

Pause, then reluctantly, "I suppose so."

"Does being helpful include finding ways to help other people use the financial data to manage their functions better?"

"It does."

"How do you feel when you are able to provide a new solution of that kind?"

"Pretty good."

"Do you think the other person, who you have helped, might perceive you as being creative?"

"I guess they might."

"So you *are* paid to be creative?"

People are often a lot more creative than they think. They simply get out of the habit of creative thought. The team coach can help them become comfortable with innovation (of which creativity is a part) by helping the team establish innovation processes that have sufficient frequency, rigour and focus; and by introducing them to a wider range of techniques that stimulate thinking from different perspectives. This is a topic worth a book on its own, so suffice it here to say that the coach can start by helping the team review its innovation process against the five basic phases of innovation management:

- **Problem definition** – what exactly is the issue? How important is it? How real is it? How committed are we to solving it? Who and what are involved?
- **Defining the process** – how does what happens happen?
- **Idea generation** – identifying alternative ways to tackle the issue.
- **Choosing between ideas** – which will give us the best and most implementable solution (the two are not necessarily the same!)?
- **Making the change happen** – planning, resourcing, championing and monitoring.

The reason for starting with the innovation process is that teams often feel more comfortable in collaborative creativity when they understand where and how it will contribute to a defined goal. Given the relatively small amount of time usually available for team coaching, creativity skills development may be best undertaken outside the coaching session. However, the practice of creativity skills is highly germane to the team coaching environment, where it can be applied to real, current issues, and it may be appropriate for the coach to introduce new techniques that are particularly effective for the type of issue in question.

Systemic thinking

Thinking systematically, which most coaches can do relatively well, is not the same as systemic thinking. Systemic thinking is about taking a holistic approach that views the team and its environment as interconnected and complex. Instead of focusing on problems and solutions, it attempts first to understand the context in which an issue is grounded. It explores the impact or influence that parts of this larger picture have on each other: what may make a change in one factor more or less effective, and what unexpected outcomes may occur.

The coach using a systemic thinking approach may help the team "map" the context of a presented issue by capturing on paper a range of factors associated with it. Some of these factors may be obvious; others may only be revealed in the flow of the learning dialogue. Headings to explore may include goals, ambitions, values, people, fears, skills, resources, self-esteem, beliefs and so on. Approaching from the presented issue, the coach might ask: "Who are all the people who have an influence on this issue and how you react to it?"

Each of these people may, if the occasion demands it, be linked to other factors in the system. For example "How does this person affect the resources available to you?" or "What values are you applying to your judgement about this person?" New factors can be added continuously as they emerge from the dialogue.

The systemic (as opposed to systematic) approach also reveals critical discontinuities. For example: "Why do you hold these values about this situation, but different values about another?" It also helps both coach and team to avoid over-simplistic analyses and solutions.

Decision making

How the team makes decisions can have a major impact on performance. Does it decide on the basis of too much or too little data? On what it knows has worked before or on what it expects might work in the future? In a participative, consultative manner or by upward delegation? With a high or low level of consensus and mutual commitment? Unfortunately, teams rarely discuss how they make decisions; the process (if there is a process) is something that just happens. By raising the issue, the team coach can help the team to explore how decision making occurs and what can be done to make it more effective.

I am grateful to Jenny Gooding and Sheryl Kennedy for introducing me to a method of profiling individual decision-making preferences and understanding how individual styles influence the team's ability to reach and implement effective decisions.[8] The keys to understanding decision-making processes lie in two observations:

- Decisions don't just happen, they result from a series of mental processes, each of which contributes to the ultimate outcome.
- Everyone pays stronger attention to some elements of this chain of thinking than to others.

Team conflict and ineffective decision making therefore result from a difference in emphasis about which steps to emphasize or from the omission of steps that are particularly important in the context of the specific decision to be made. At the basic level, there are three phases of decision making:

- **Attending to the potential for action** – which includes recognizing that there is a problem or requirement for a decision, trying to understand it and generating possible solutions or tactics.
- **Intending to take action** – which includes working out what needs to be done, showing resolve or persistence to pursue the decision, and evaluating what is important.
- **Committing to action** – which includes timing (choosing the right time to act and pacing action appropriately) and anticipating the progress and impact of action.

Altogether, the decision-making process entails 12 different steps. A revelation for me, for example, was that although I am regarded as highly creative in how I approach problems, my preference is strongly skewed towards extrapolating and linking concepts, rather than towards generating off-the-wall ideas.

Just as teams need to be aware of their preferences in terms of task-achievement (doing) roles and shaping the outcome, so it helps if they understand their collective strengths and weaknesses in terms of decision making. Valuing all the steps in decision making (and hence individual preferences) and ensuring that all steps are managed effectively can potentially make a huge contribution to team effectiveness.

Key questions the coach might ask include:

- What are our collective style preferences in decision making?
- What kinds of decision are best/least suited to this style preference?
- How do the individual differences in preference affect how we work together? How we set and manage priorities? How we value each other's contributions?
- What do we want to change about how we make decisions as a team?

Communication

It is ironic that the explosion in communications (the technology of communication) has led to so little improvement in communication (the sharing of understanding and meaning and the building of relationships). Especially in virtual teams, it is vital to ensure that communication balances the transactional and the relational interactions.

Once again, the team coach can help by providing a framework around which the team can build its dialogue on the management of communication. One such framework identifies three levels of team interaction, each of which may need a separate approach in terms of frequency, timing, style and process:

- **Strategic communication** is about planning ahead. It requires the team to come together at infrequent but regular intervals to assess whether what it is doing and intends to do still fits the environment in which it operates. It also requires ongoing *ad hoc* dialogue in between, to reach agreement and understanding about minor changes of direction.

- **Coordinating communication** is about managing the inter-dependencies, ensuring that people have the information they need to pace and integrate their work with that of other team members.
- **Autonomous communication** is needed when people do tasks on their own (e.g. doctors who have their own case load), but share thoughts and experiences that they think will be of help to colleagues, or to gain support and advice from colleagues, or simply because they need to maintain the social linkages.

Most teams need all three levels of interaction. The coach can stimulate the dialogue that identifies how well each of these levels is working, and how it could be improved.

COMMUNICATION AND FEEDBACK IN A CHILEAN TELEVISION COMPANY

One of the five television broadcasters in Chile was undergoing substantial structural changes across the organization and among the top team during 2001 and 2002. The top management group needed to become more focused and more effective to overcome eight years of losses – they had to begin working together as a genuine team. In particular, they needed to develop more clearly defined goals, to build the quality of communication and trust, and align operations between some areas of the business.

Coach Rodrigo Lara and a colleague worked with both individual senior executives and the team as a whole. One of the first tasks was to educate them about what an effective team looks like, by introducing them to authors such as Katzenbach and Smith. Other interventions included workshops where the team used coaching dialogue to explore business and interpersonal issues; and outdoor events to help them build relationships and reflect on issues in a different environment.

Maintaining the mixture of individual and team coaching was one of the most useful but also most difficult tasks. On the positive side, it helped the coach check information and perceptions. On the negative, the coach had to be very careful in using information and in keeping an equal distance from all the members, because some of those whom they were not coaching individually might have perceived the coach to be closer to those members whom they were coaching one to one.

Coaching interventions took two forms. In one, the whole team met off-site in a hotel, to address issues such as communication, trust and sharing knowledge. In the other, they met in the office as normal to discuss technical issues and the coach observed, commented and facilitated.

Feedback – from each other and from the coaches – played an important role in initiating and sustaining learning conversations. It also helped build the level of trust the team needed to cope with the major challenges facing the business. At first, one of the key members of the team was highly suspicious of the coaches and others were reluctant to be fully open. As the benefits become clear, however, the coaches needed to cope with the opposite problem: over-high expectations, resulting from team members attributing too much of the business success to the coaching rather than to their own efforts. The team occasionally relapsed into old behaviours; Lara describes this as a spiral process of development, maturing and partial regression that triggered a further bout of mutual development.

Other issues for the coaches included helping the team overcome the initial pessimism created by such a long period of poor business performance; helping people recognize, value and learn from each other's complementary skills; and using real, current problems as the foundation for team building. An item of learning for Lara was that the team achieved more when the coach appeared to do less. The solutions that emerged were better when the coaches allowed the team to develop its own solutions than when they succumbed to temptation and made suggestions of their own.

The team's confidence in its own ability rose gradually from low self-expectations in 2001 and by the end of that year the company broke even. Since then it has been the industry profit leader, taking fully 50 per cent of the total profit of the sector in 2004.

The coaches worked with the team as a whole for eight days each over the first year, gradually reducing the frequency of interventions, until by 2004 the team had the confidence and capability to coach itself and no longer needed external intervention. Regular impact measured by interviews and surveys every six months identified both individual and team changes.

Written by Rodrigo Lara, a partner at MAS Consultores, a Chilean human resources consultancy. Rodrigo can be contacted at rlara@masconsultores.cl.

Evaluating the impact of team coaching

Team coaching may be thought-provoking and motivational, but what specific benefits have accrued as a result? (Or put another way, what has changed for the better that is important in terms of achieving the team task?)

Both individual and team coaching affect a number of stakeholders: individual team members, the team as a whole, sub-groups within the team, the organization and other teams. They also affect both **process** (how the team and the individuals do things) and **outcomes** (the results of what they do). It therefore helps to think about evaluation in terms of a balanced portfolio, as illustrated in Table 5.2 overleaf. Process improvements may be interpersonal, informational (communication) or technical.

A factor not included in this table as an item in its own right is the learning that underlies each of these process improvements and outcomes. It can be helpful in the overall evaluation to begin the coaching intervention with an analysis of the learning that each stakeholder expects or would like to achieve, using the same

TABLE 5.2

EVALUATING TEAM COACHING

STAKEHOLDER	PROCESS IMPROVEMENTS	SAMPLE OUTCOMES
Individual	Interpersonal, e.g. increased confidence Information, e.g. knowing what knowledge resources are within the team Technical, e.g. improved computer skills	Achieving sales target/annual bonus Higher personal productivity
Team	Interpersonal, e.g. reduced negative conflict Informational, e.g. more efficient communication between office-based and field-based staff Technical, e.g. smooth introduction of new software system	Improved customer satisfaction ratings Higher team productivity Reduced cost of quality
Sub-group	Interpersonal, e.g. reduced negative conflict with other sub-groups Informational, e.g. improved liaison with other sub-groups Technical, e.g. reduced problems with hand-overs within the team	Improved contribution to specific team goals
Organization	Interpersonal, e.g. improved team reputation Informational, e.g. improved reporting systems Technical, e.g. development of systems and approaches that can be used more widely in the organization	Bottom-line impact Customer retention

TABLE 5.2 (CONT.)

STAKEHOLDER	PROCESS IMPROVEMENTS	SAMPLE OUTCOMES
Other teams	Interpersonal, e.g. less inter-team conflict Information, e.g. significant flow of knowledge/ good practice to other teams and into the team Technical, e.g. reduced handover problems	Reduced cost of quality

headings as in Table 5.2. This record can then be compared with the learning actually achieved, at mid-point reviews and at the end of the coaching programme. Like task achievements, learning achievements can also be seen in terms of process (what we have learned that helps us do things better) and outputs (how we have applied the learning).

Expect the unexpected

As promised, this chapter has ranged widely in the themes covered. That reflects the reality of the team coach's role. It is very hard to predict what aspects the team may need help with; the team coach simply has to expect the unexpected. In almost all cases, however, the issues that arise will have a team dimension, a number of individual dimensions and an organizational dimension. So whenever the team needs to focus on one area, it is highly probable that other issues will also be relevant at the same time.

The next chapter looks at how the team can continue the coaching process even without the hands-on help of the coach. However, teams where the coach is embedded, or which are not yet ready to coach themselves, need to develop through the levels of learning maturity explored in Chapter 4. The coach can help them incorporate in the planning process the steps and resources that will build both individual and team capacity for learning and take it to the level of learning team that it desires to be.

FINAL COACHING QUESTION

What is your process for expanding the range of team-related issues on which you can be confident in helping a team reflect in a structured and purposeful manner?

CHAPTER SIX

The self-coaching team

"Life is but an endless series of experiments." | **Mahatma Gandhi**

I t's easy to get hooked on the role of team coach. It's great to be wanted, appreciated and to see a group of people coalesce into a genuine, high-performing team. But a core competence for the effective team coach is knowing when to back off and leave the team to its own devices. Failure to do so risks creating an unhealthy dependence. This is as true for the line manager coach as for the external team coach. Of course, there may always be new challenges for which the team may welcome a coaching input; but the coach is now an occasional visitor, by invitation.

In order for the coach to be able to back off, the team has to absorb and be confident in sustaining the coaching processes from its internal resources. It also needs to be able to recognize when, occasionally, it may be better to request the coach to intervene again – perhaps to review and enhance its self-coaching skills in the light of specific new demands on the team.

Managing the transition to self-coaching

In preparing the team for this new phase of coaching, the team coach needs to set out clearly at an early stage the nature of this transition, the reasons for it and how it will be managed. If the team is

BEING COACHED VERSUS SELF-COACHING

BEING COACHED	SELF-COACHING
The coach: Asks the difficult questions Points the way to new knowledge Defines and leads the coaching process Observes and gives feedback Motivates learning through praise and the "Pygmalion" effect	*The team:* Finds the difficult questions, wherever they are Tracks down new knowledge Adapts and leads the coaching process Generates its own feedback, internally and from others Motivates itself to learn

sufficiently mature in its learning processes, the coach may invite its members to design the transition process.

It helps to be clear from the start about the difference between a team that is being coached and one that is coaching itself, so that everyone has a shared vision of this important transition and is able to contribute to the discussion of how it will be achieved. The transition itself is unlikely to be abrupt. More progress will be made on some fronts than others and, like any other behavioural change, there will be false starts and relapses. Table 6.1 indicates some of the most significant characteristics of the transition.

Finding their own difficult questions

New questions arise from new perspectives. The team members need to develop the ability to see issues differently and to ensure that they are constantly supplied with different perspectives from the external world. Among practical steps the team can take are:

◆ Gathering feedback from customers and other stakeholders, based on the two questions: "What would we find it useful for them to tell us?" and "What would they like to tell us?"

- Benchmarking against other teams and organizations – what do they do that we don't?
- Building its own library of good, relevant coaching questions, questions that experience tells it will stimulate useful dialogue. One way to generate new such questions is to approach new issues with "What is the coaching question?"

In the book *Coaching at Work*,[1] David Megginson and I pointed out:

> "The purpose of learning dialogue is not to find a better answer. It is to find a better question. From a better question flows a stream of possibilities, in which better answers are eddies on the journey to discovery."

Focusing constantly on finding the right answer can be highly unproductive. Even if a right answer does exist in the murky world of management and technology, it is only a matter of time before a new answer is required. The coach can leave the team with a full basket of good coaching questions to set it off on its solo journey, but it is even more important to help develop the skill within the team to ask its own coaching questions.

Tracking down new knowledge

New knowledge is everywhere, if only you know where to look. Practical steps to do so include:

- Improving the networking skills of the team, so that other people and other teams bring it into their knowledge pools.
- Encouraging team members to participate in teams outside their base team. For example, making sure that every member of a stable team is attached at least once a year to a project group drawn from several teams.

◆ Actively seeking out and taking part in web-based communities of interest, not just in the immediate area of interest of the team, but in peripheral or parallel areas that may give rise to new ideas and practices.

The key here is to ensure that these activities are sustainable, by building them into the daily or weekly routine and demonstrating that they are valued.

Taking over the coaching process

The leaders of effective learning teams focus more on creating the climate where coaching can flourish than on doing coaching. For the team to internalize the coaching process, the members need to be reasonably adept in the roles of both coach and coachee. It also helps to establish ground rules, such as:

◆ Everyone has a responsibility to coach and be coached, when the need and opportunity arise.
◆ Team members should be open about their coaching needs and take the initiative in seeking coaching, both within the team and from outside experts.
◆ The team will review the quality of its coaching regularly.
◆ The team development plan will address continuous improvement in coaching capability.

Generating feedback

Learning teams have sufficient psychological safety for members to offer open, honest and timely feedback to each other. But the opportunity may often be lost because people are very busy, or don't have frequent opportunities to interact. It's important, therefore, to build in specific opportunities to generate feedback.

Opportunities might be created, for example:

◆ At the mid point and end point of projects
◆ At or just before regular team meetings (whether face to face or virtual)
◆ In regular forums set up for the sole purpose of seeking improvement in managing task, learning and behaviour

Self-motivated learning

The enthusiasm for planned learning can be hard to sustain in the typical workplace, with its incessant pressures and distractions. The coach can help the team develop the skills to assess and review its learning motivation and to recognize and react when individuals begin to lose their learning motivation. Regular review of the team motivational climate (in terms of both task performance and learning) is a simple and practical aid. It is sometimes useful as part of this review process to explore the underlying mood of the team. Are we broadly optimistic or pessimistic? Hopeful or despairing? Cautious or adventurous? And what do we need to do to change the underlying mood?

Table 6.2 overleaf provides a simple but effective way of assessing the team's learning motivation.

Creating the environment for the self-coaching team

Once these basics are in place, or at least in train as part of the transition from being coached to self-coaching, the self-coaching team needs to develop a sustainable capability to:

◆ Balance the focus on task, learning and behaviour
◆ Create frequent opportunities for learning dialogue, both formal and informal

TABLE 6.2

ASSESSING LEARNING MOTIVATION

HIGH LEARNING MOTIVATION

- We always see lots of opportunities to learn from what we are doing, from each other, from sources outside the team
- We enjoy learning new things and doing new things
- Learning is worthwhile for its own sake

MODERATE LEARNING MOTIVATION

- We see limited opportunities for learning from our work
- We enjoy having opportunities to discuss and learn, when and if we have the time
- Learning is worthwhile when it can be immediately applied

LOW LEARNING MOTIVATION

- We're too busy getting the job done to worry about learning from it
- If we've got time to spare, the last thing we want to talk about is anything relating to our work
- We're not really interested in learning more than we need simply to do the job

---

- Feel comfortable with the uncomfortable
- Manage the team learning process
- Establish the protective mechanisms that prevent external influences – such as high stress-inducing demands for greater output – from derailing learning plans

Balance the focus on task, learning and behaviour

Without a counterbalancing force, most teams will naturally gravitate towards task activities at the expense of reflection and learning. As part of regular team meetings, it helps to ask the following coaching questions:

- What learning opportunities did we miss?
- What behaviours interfered with getting the job done?
- What did we do that we didn't need to do?
- What have we added to our collective capability?

Create frequent opportunities for learning dialogue, both formal and informal

Effective learning teams don't wait for six-monthly team-building events to binge on learning. They expect learning dialogue to occur wherever an opportunity arises. That includes chance conversations at the coffee machine, formal team meetings, one-to-one coaching sessions, project meetings and so on.

NO WORRIES!

One company uses the first two hours of its monthly all-day top team meeting to split into co-coaching pairs. It finds that the quality of the subsequent meeting is vastly improved, because the team members have got rid of many of the worries that would otherwise have distracted them.

Feel comfortable with the uncomfortable

Like athletes constantly pushing themselves through the pain barrier to achieve ever greater performance, the team and its members need to overcome the natural fear of tackling difficult issues of real or potential conflict, expanding their tolerance for ambiguity and constructive confrontation. The skills to initiate and manage difficult conversations are invaluable, especially in teams with a culturally diverse membership. Being able to practise these skills within the team, in a relatively safe environment, builds valuable capacity to manage the interfaces between the team and the external environment.

Manage the team learning process

The experience of effective learning teams is generally that the quality and quantity of the learning that takes place are influenced by how seriously the leader, in particular, takes the process of managing team learning. Without this attention, learning tends either to be focused on individuals and undistributed, or is spasmodic, confined mainly to times when the task pressures are low. Building learning routines into the day-to-day, week-to-week structure of team activities makes learning a continuous, fluid activity.

Protect team learning from external derailers

Especially in matrixed organizations, teams are prone to sudden, unreasonable demands on their time, attention and resources. It's all too easy for learning to be relegated to a low priority. Part of the problem is that what is promoted as a short-term switch of emphasis all too easily becomes the norm. If the team has a high level of clarity about its effective capacity, however, it may be more able to resist unreasonable demands by applying a coaching perspective. For example:

◆ Asking what the team should stop doing, in order to make room for the new requirements.
◆ Engaging with the clients to develop a deeper understanding on both sides of the implications of what is being asked for.
◆ Linking the demands on the team with both broader organizational priorities and organizational values.

There is, of course, no panacea and some pressures can't be resisted. But a continuous coaching conversation can help the team determine what it can control, what it can influence and what it will just plain have to live with – and somewhere in the crevices of these three areas there will normally be spaces for continued learning.

How team learning roles support the self-coaching team

The concept of team roles has been popular in team building since the 1970s. Two main instruments are widely used today: those by Belbin[2] and Margerison-McCann.[3] However, the concept of **team learning roles** emerged only gradually within our study of team learning. Belbin and others evolved their team roles by observing how various teams achieved task goals, on the assumption that task achievement is the sole significant *raison d'être* of a team. This view can be strongly challenged. Teams may have a number of contiguous purposes, of which task achievement is but one. Socialization (kinship) and learning are obvious other goals that the team may simultaneously maintain.

From the experiences of participants in our research into team learning, it was clear that they or people who had helped them had played a number of different developmental roles, expressed in Figures 6.1 and 6.2.

Figure 6.1 is based on two dimensions: challenging versus nurturing (i.e. the degree to which the intention is to stretch the team and its members versus the intention to support and encourage); and doing (action) versus reflecting.

These dimensions give rise to four roles:

- **Motivator** – providing the vision and the enthusiasm from which shared learning goals arise.
- **Skills coach** – helping other team members acquire skills and knowledge.
- **Reviewer** – ensuring that the team takes time to reflect and engage in learning dialogue.
- **Question-raiser** – ensuring that issues that need to be the subject of discussion and dialogue are raised at appropriate times.

FIGURE 6.1

TEAM ROLES FOR DEVELOPMENT

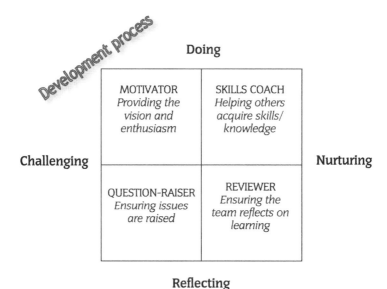

	Doing	
	MOTIVATOR *Providing the vision and enthusiasm*	**SKILLS COACH** *Helping others acquire skills/ knowledge*
	QUESTION-RAISER *Ensuring issues are raised*	**REVIEWER** *Ensuring the team reflects on learning*

Challenging — Nurturing

Reflecting

Figure 6.2 is concerned with the other side of the learning coin: the process of gathering knowledge, from which learning is derived. The dimensions here are external versus internal (whether the knowledge source is within the team or outside it); and formal versus informal (whether the role has to be part of a visible or approved structure or system).

The four resultant roles can be described as:

- **Gateway to permission/information** – gaining the organization's agreement to experiment, spend money on training and so on, plus access to formally held information, which may or may not be generally available.
- **Gateway to knowledge** – using informal networks to access other people's expertise and experience outside the team.
- **Specialist** – becoming a knowledge resource in one or more areas (usually areas that other people weren't interested in but that proved invaluable from time to time, for example having

FIGURE 6.2

TEAM LEARNING ROLES FOR KNOWLEDGE GATHERING

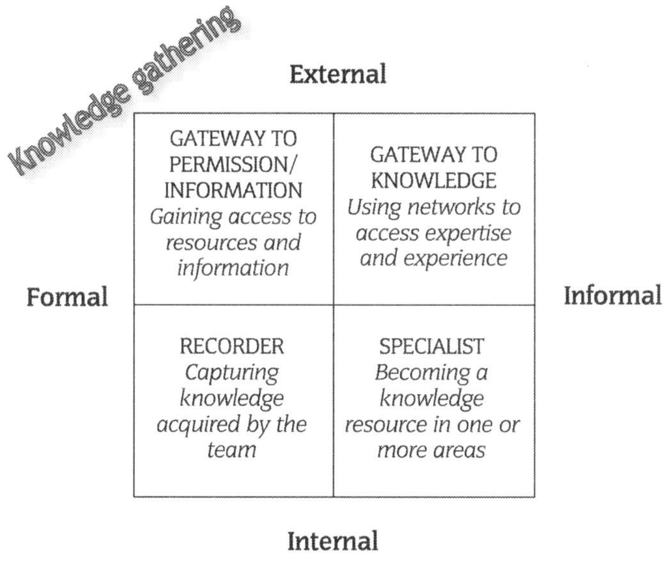

Knowledge gathering

External

GATEWAY TO PERMISSION/ INFORMATION *Gaining access to resources and information*	GATEWAY TO KNOWLEDGE *Using networks to access expertise and experience*
RECORDER *Capturing knowledge acquired by the team*	SPECIALIST *Becoming a knowledge resource in one or more areas*

Formal   **Informal**

Internal

someone in the team who knows what to do when a computer crashes).

◆ **Recorder** – capturing and recording knowledge acquired by the team and/or its members, so that it can be made available both within the team and to other teams.

These various roles were surprisingly common and consistent among the more learning-oriented teams we investigated. People played a variety of roles according to need and circumstance, and were surprisingly flexible in their range of team learning roles, but inevitably preferred or were more at home with some roles rather than others. We have subsequently found all of the roles being played in all of the six types of team, but without a consistent pattern as to which are most important. It seems that teams that learn most effectively use all of the roles, though not necessarily all at the same time. Whether these learning roles also have an impact on team task performance is an unanswered question – more research needs to be done and the impact is likely to be indirect (i.e. a moderating factor rather than a direct source of cause and effect).

High-performance teams also seem to be more likely to value each of the team learning roles, to encourage people to undertake them and to recognize their efforts in doing so. The pay-offs in terms of learning appear to be increased depth and durability of team knowledge; reinforcement of the habits of continuous, planned learning by individuals and the team; and more rigorous, consistent team learning processes.

The self-coaching team and succession planning

As a result of their learning focus, learning teams often have a reputation and track record as breeding grounds for talent. Succession planning is normally seen as focused on individuals, yet it is rare for an individual's achievements or failures to be solely due to their own efforts. In the learning team, people add to each other's reputations. By developing effective team learning behaviours, the team can provide a safe environment for nurturing talent. Indeed, it is quite common to find that organizations second to the learning team talented people who have been identified in other departments or functions; or target members of the learning team as coaches to people in other teams.

In a few cases, learning teams have been tasked with the development of a high flyer in their first managerial role: managing them upwards. This explicit reversal of the normal coaching role – the team coaching the new manager – is a sign of the team's learning maturity and potentially a powerful grounding for the managerial recruit. (This kind of upward coaching has, of course, occurred in the armed forces for hundreds of years.)

Learning to coach other teams

PILOT STORES TO TRANSFER LEARNING

One of the most effective transfers of learning I have observed took place in the supermarket chain ASDA, which used a small number of stores to pilot new ways of managing employee communication. Each of the pilot stores experimented with the help of external consultants, gradually building up experience in what did and didn't work. Typically, the new procedures would then have been rolled out by the human resources department and the consultants. Instead, ASDA opted to train teams from the pilot stores to be the ambassadors and coaches to the rest of the organization. Because these people did the job day in day out, they were far more credible than outsiders or people from headquarters – and hence far more effective at overcoming resistance to new ways of doing things.

One of the bonuses of coaching and mentoring is that they undermine the idea – so fixed in the mentality of many organizations – that you have to be an educational or training expert to help someone else to learn. (It's probably true that you need to be an expert to *teach*, which is why most universities are institutes of teaching rather than institutions of learning!) Although the "corporate universities" that have sprung up in many large organizations in recent years are populated mainly by experts in training or education, the pioneers of the corporate university had a very different model. Their faculties were composed of senior managers and experienced professionals and they encouraged everyone at that level to view themselves as a source of learning for anyone in the organization. In time, they realized that people at other levels also had great potential to act as coaches, both informally and within the structure of the corporate faculty.

Particularly with the advent of electronic coaching, the potential for teams to coach other teams, or for sub-groups within teams to coach their counterparts elsewhere, is vast.

TWO-WAY LEARNING

A European company that had acquired a factory in China invested in teaching key teams in the acquisition to understand and converse in English. It then paired these teams with English-speaking teams doing a similar manufacturing task in Europe. Once a month, each team would attend the meetings of its counterpart by videoconference. The Chinese teams were able to learn both by gaining advice and feedback from the Europeans, and by observing the problems that the Europeans were wrestling with. Eventually, the flow of learning became two-way (as it always should in mentoring and often does in coaching).

Another organization that has recognized that expertise doesn't just rest with the experts is the UK's National Health Service. Its Expert Patient scheme includes coaching by patients for health professionals. The same principle can be applied to coaching and mentoring within commercial organizations. We have already seen a rapid growth of "upward mentoring", where relatively junior mentors help executives understand the realities of diversity, or of what actually happens at the customer interface. There is no good reason why top management should not create a similar learning arrangement with a team at the sharp end of the business – other than fear, perhaps.

Useful coaching questions to help the team consider its role as a coaching team include:

◆ What's in it for us? How will we ensure that we receive the recognition and support we need? Will it give us greater licence to experiment and do we want that?

- What knowledge and skills do we have that could be useful to other teams?
- How can we create the kind of relationship with other teams where we can share our learning without making them resentful?
- How can we capture our learning in ways that make it easier to transfer to others?
- Where will we find the resources (particularly time) to help others in this way?
- How will we ensure that these coaching conversations involve two-way learning?

Handing over the coaching process

What can the coach do to make the transition to self-coaching both smooth and effective? Some basic ground rules are outlined below.

Prepare the ground at an early stage

It's very easy for the relationship between the coach and the team to become cosy. The more reliant the team becomes on the coach to ask the difficult questions, to raise issues at the right time, to facilitate the management of real or potential conflict, the more difficult it will be to step aside. Putting a time frame on the coaching programme (e.g. "We only have six meetings, so let's make the most of them") helps; so do clarifying at the beginning what success of the coaching intervention will look like and using the mid-point review meeting(s) to reinforce the expectation of ending.

Excite the team about doing things for itself

Making self-sufficiency a team goal is an explicit way of managing expectations. Useful questions include:

◆ What would it feel like to do this without support?
◆ What would it take to ensure that this kind of dialogue happens naturally within the team, whenever it is needed?
◆ What is our vision of coaching self-sufficiency?

Transfer ownership of process along with ownership of solutions

One of the worst coaches I have observed treated his clients in much the same way as a stage magician treats the stooges from the audience. He had a box of clever tricks (he'd been on a neurolinguistic programming course) and got his kicks from the client's admiration of his technique. Although he did, to be fair, establish some good insights, there was no doubt who was in charge of the process. Moreover, he believed that it was better that the process should remain a mystery to the client, because they would lose the naturalness of their response.

What this coach failed to see was that coaching is most effective when it is a collaborative endeavour. The coachee (whether individual or team) will only truly grow when the power is vested in them. The power of the relationship rests in turn on two factors: who owns the goals and who owns the process. Empowering coaching is done *with* the learner not *to* the learner. So there are strong arguments for explaining the coaching processes and techniques being used, gaining the coachee's consent to use them, and teaching them how to manage these processes both within the coaching dialogue and when the coach is not there, in the form of self-coaching.

In explaining the coaching process, the coach will need to cover:

- What the approach or technique is intended to achieve
- Its pluses and minuses in use (using real examples if possible)
- The theory and/or psychology behind it
- When it typically works and doesn't work
- How to find out more about the approach (e.g. through further reading)

Where time and opportunity exist, the coach can also provide an opportunity for the team to practise the technique, perhaps on less important issues. I have occasionally invited a team to coach me on an issue, as a non-threatening practice opportunity, and found that this reinforces their confidence.

Equip the team to find multiple sources of support and reflection in the future

No team is an island, to misquote an old saw. The objective of achieving self-coaching capability is not that the team should never need external help and advice again. But it should have a much clearer idea of how to get and use external support from a much wider range of sources.

Useful coaching questions include:

- Who could stimulate our thinking and provide different perspectives?
- What are the critical support relationships we need to build/maintain and who in the team is responsible for maintaining them?
- How will we gain and preserve internal and external legitimacy for creating team reflective space?
- When and how will we recognize situations where targeted coaching will be valuable for us in future?
- Who should we be coaching in turn?

This last point is a reflection of team learning maturity. Being confident and capable enough to take coaching to other teams and even, if the environment is right, to more senior management is a sure sign of a team that has itself been well coached. It may take time to reach this pinnacle, but it is an exhilarating place to be, both for the team and for the coach who helped it get there.

The ultimate goal

This chapter has taken us to the ultimate goal of coaching: the relative self-sufficiency that comes from the team having the skills, motivation and environment in which it can apply coaching techniques with skill and insight to its own issues, in its own way and in its own time.

FINAL COACHING QUESTION

What is your vision of the ideal handover to the team and what do you need to do to realize that vision?

Notes

Introduction

1 See D. Clutterbuck and D. Megginson (2004) *Coaching at Work: Creating a Coaching Culture*, CIPD, Wimbledon.

2 P. Senge (1999) "Why organizations still aren't learning", *Training*, Sept: 41–9.

Chapter 1

1 D. Anderson and M. Anderson (2005) *Coaching that Counts*, Elsevier, Oxford.

2 M. Landsberg (1996) *The Tao of Coaching*, HarperCollins, London.

3 M. Thier (2003) *Coaching Clues*, Nicholas Brealey Publishing, London.

4 For an article expanding on these dangers, read S. Berglas (2002) "The very real dangers of executive coaching", *Harvard Business Review*, 80(6): 86–92.

5 For more about Socratic dialogue, see www.sfcp.org.uk/socratic-dialogue.html.

6 Berglas, *op. cit.*

7 A.M. Grant and J. Greene (2004) *Coach Yourself: Make Real Changes in Your Life* (2nd edn), Momentum Press, London.

8 J. Whitmore (1996) *Coaching for Performance*, Nicholas Brealey Publishing, London.

9 C. Argyris and D. Schon (1974) *Theory in Practice: Increasing Professional Effectiveness*, Jossey-Bass, San Francisco; (1978)

Organizational Learning: A Theory of Action Perspective, Addison Wesley, Reading, MA.

10 These are explored in more detail in D. Megginson and D. Clutterbuck (2005) *Techniques for Coaching and Mentoring*, Elsevier, Oxford.

Chapter 2

1   See R.H. Franke and J.D. Kaul (1978) "The Hawthorne experiments: First statistical interpretation", *American Sociological Review*, 43: 623–43.

2   J.R. Hackman (1990) *Groups that Work (and Those that Don't): Creating Conditions for Effective Teamwork*, Jossey-Bass, San Francisco.

3   J.R. Katzenbach and D.K. Smith (1999) *The Wisdom of Teams: Creating the High-Performance Organization*, London: HarperBusiness.

4   L. Thompson (2000) *Making the Team: A Guide for Managers*, Prentice Hall, Upper Saddle River, NJ.

5   J.R. Hackman (1990) "Introduction: Work teams in organizations: An oriented framework", in Hackman, *op. cit.*

6   J. Margolis (1999) "Playing by the rules", paper presented to Academy of Management Annual Meeting, Chicago.

7   D. Clutterbuck (1999) *Doing It Different*, Orion, London.

8   M.J. Hatch and K. Weick (1998) "Critical resistance to the jazz metaphor", *Organization Science*, 9(5): 600–4.

9   J.R. Hackman (1987) "The design of work teams", in J.W. Lorsch (ed.) *Handbook of Organizational Behavior*, Prentice Hall, Upper Saddle River, NJ.

10 D. Clutterbuck and S. Kernaghan (1994) *The Power of Empowerment*, Kogan Page, London, pp 39–44.

11 A. Edmondson (1999) "Psychological safety and learning behavior in teams", *Administrative Science Quarterly*, 44: 350–83.

12 R. Ratliff, S.M. Beckstead and S.H. Hanke (1999) "The use and management of teams: A how-to guide", *Quality Progress*, June.

13 J. Olson and K.M. Branch (2002) "Teams and project- and program-based organizations", provisional chapter for unpublished book.

14 M. Ringelmann (1913) *Aménagement des fumiers et des purins*, Librairie Agricole de la Maison Rustique, Paris.

15 J.R. Katzenbach (1998) *Teams at the Top: Unleashing the Potential of Both Teams and Individual Leaders*, Harvard Business School Press, Boston.

16 K.A. Bantel and S.E. Jackson (1989) "Top management and innovations in banking: Does composition of the top team make a difference?" *Strategic Management Journal*, 10: 107–12; A.I. Murray (1989) "Top management group heterogeneity and firm performance", *Strategic Management Journal*, 10: 125–41.

17 A.C. Amason (1996) "Distinguishing the effects of functional and dysfunctional conflict on strategic decision-making: Resolving a paradox for top management teams", *Academy of Management Journal*, 39(1): 123–48.

18 B. Woolrudeg and S.W. Floyd (1990) "The strategy process, middle management involvement and organizational performance", *Strategic Management Journal*, 11: 231–41.

19 For example, P.C. Early and E. Mosakowski (2000) "Creating hybrid team cultures: An empirical test of transnational team functioning", *Academy of Management Journal*, 43(1): 26–49.

20 E. Elron, B. Shamir and E. Ben-Ari (1998) "Why don't they fight each other? Cultural diversity and operational unity in multinational forces", working paper, Hebrew University, Jerusalem.

21 M. Bergami and R.P. Bagozzi (2000) "Self-categorization, affective commitment, and group self-esteem as distinct aspects of social identity in the organization", *British Journal of Social Psychology*, 39: 555–77.

22 Early and Mosakowski, *op. cit.*

23 G.S. Van der Vegt and J.S. Bunderson (2005) "Learning and performance in multidisciplinary teams: The importance of collective team identification", *Academy of Management Journal*, 48(3): 532–47; K.L. Bettenhausen (1991) "Five years of groups research: What we have learned and what needs to be addressed", *Journal of Management*, 17(2): 345–81; W. Wood (1987) "Meta-analytic review of sex differences in group performance", *Simulation and Games*, 19: 82–98.

24 J.L. Hale and F.J. Boster (1988) "Comparing effect coded models of choice shifts", *Communication Research Reports*, 5: 180–6.

25 L.L. Gilson and C.E. Shalley (2004) "A little creativity goes a long way: An examination of teams' engagement in creative processes", *Journal of Management*, 30: 453–70.

26 T.M. Amabile (1996) *Creativity in Context*, Westview Press, Boulder, CO; R.W. Woodman, J.E. Sawyer and R.W. Griffin (1993) "Toward a theory of organizational creativity", *Academy of Management Review*, 18: 293–332.

27 L. Gilson, J. Matthieu, G. Shalley and T. Ruddy (2005) "Creativity and standardization: Complementary or conflicting drivers of team effectiveness?" *Academy of Management Journal*, 48(3): 521–31.

28 J.D. Olian and S.L. Rynes (1991) "Making total quality work: Aligning organizational processes, performance measures and stakeholders", *Human Resource Management*, 30: 303–33.

29 Gilson *et al.*, *op. cit.*

30 J. Barker (1993) "Tightening the iron cage: Concertive control in self-managing teams", *Administrative Science Quarterly*, 38: 408–37.

31 R. Wageman (1995) "Interdependence and group effectiveness", *Administrative Science Quarterly*, 40: 145–80.

32 R. Madhavan and R. Grover (1998) "From embedded knowledge to embodied knowledge: New product development as knowledge management", *Journal of Marketing*, 62(4): 1–12.

33 D.G. Ancona (1990) "Outward bound: Strategies for team survival in the organization", *Academy of Management Journal*, 33: 334–65; D.G. Ancona and D.F. Caldwell (1988) "Beyond task and maintenance: Defining external functions in groups", *Group and Organizational Studies*, 13: 488–94.

34 D.G. Ancona and D.F. Caldwell (1992) "Bridging the boundary; External activity and performance in organizational teams", *Administrative Science Quarterly*, 37: 634–65.

35 C. Argyris (1962) *Interpersonal Competence and Organizational Effectiveness*, Dorsey, Homewood, IL; B.M. Staw, L.E. Sandelands and J.E. Dutton (1981) "Threat-rigidity effects in organizational behavior: A multilevel analysis", *Administrative Science Quarterly*, 26: 501–24; I.J. Roseman, C. Wiest and T.S. Swartz (1994) "Phenomenology, behaviors and goals differentiate discrete emotions", *Journal of Personal and Social Psychology*, 67: 206–21.

36 L.H. Pelled (1996) "Demographic diversity, conflict and work group outcomes: An intervening process theory", *Organization Science*, 7: 615–31.

37 R.A. Baron (1990) "Countering the effects of destructive criticism: The relative efficacy of four interventions", *Journal of Applied Psychology*, 75: 235–45.

38 D. Schweiger, W. Sandberg and P. Rechner (1989) "Experiential effects of dialectical enquiry, devil's advocacy and consensus approaches to strategic decision-making", *Academy of Management Journal*, 32: 745–72.

39 I.L. Janis (1982) *Groupthink*, Houghton-Mifflin, Boston.

40 C. Schwenk and J.S. Valacich (1994) "Effects of devil's advocacy and dialectical enquiry on individuals versus groups", *Organizational Behavior and Human Decision Processes*, 59: 210–22; K.A. Jehn (1995) "A multimethod examination of the benefits and detriments of intergroup conflict", *Administrative Science Quarterly*, 40: 256–82.

41 R.A. Baron (1991) "Positive effects of conflict: A cognitive perspective", *Employee Responsibilities and Rights Journal*, 4: 25–36.

42 L.L. Putnam (1994) "Proactive conflict: Negotiation as implicit coordination", *International Journal of Conflict Management*, 5: 285–99.

43 D. Tjosvold, V. Dann and C. Wong (1992) "Managing conflict between departments to serve customers", *Human Relations*, 45: 13–23.

44 J.K. Murnighan and D.E. Conlon (1991) "The dynamics of intense work groups: A study of British string quartets", *Administrative Science Quarterly*, 36: 165–86.

45 K.A. Jehn (1995) "A multimethod examination of the benefits and detriments of intragroup conflict", *Administrative Science Quarterly*, 40: 256–82.

46 K. John (1992) "The impact of intragroup conflict on effectiveness: A multi-method examination of the benefits and detriments of conflict", doctoral dissertation Northwestern University, IL; K. John (1997) "A qualitative analysis of conflict types and dimensions in organizational groups", *Administrative Science Quarterly*, 42: 540–57.

47 K.A. Jehn and E.A. Mannix (2001) "The dynamic nature of conflict: A longitudinal study of intragroup conflict and group performance", *Academy of Management Journal*, 44(2): 238–51.

48 *Ibid*.

49 A. Amason (1996) "Distinguishing the effects of functional and dysfunctional conflict on strategic decision making: Resolving a paradox for top management teams", *Academy of Management Journal*, 39(1): 123–48; D.M. Schweiger, W.R. Sandberg and J.W. Ragan (1986) "Group approaches for improving strategic decision-making: A comparative study of dialectical inquiry, devil's advocacy and consensus approaches to strategic decision-making", *Academy of Management Journal*, 29: 51–71.

50 A. Mant (1983) *The Leaders You Deserve*, Blackwell, Oxford.

51 R. Corn (2000) "Why poor teams get poorer: The influence of team effectiveness and design quality on the quality of group

diagnostic processes", unpublished doctoral thesis, Harvard University, Cambridge, MA; K.K. Smith and D.N. Berg (1987) *Paradoxes of Group Life*, Jossey-Bass, San Francisco.

52 S.A. Haslam, C. McGarty, P.M. Brown, R.A. Eggins, B.E. Morrison and K.J. Reynolds (1998) "Inspecting the emperor's clothes: Evidence that random selection of leaders can enhance group performance", *Group Dynamics: Theory, Research and Practice*, 2(3): 168–84.

53 M. Hoegl and H.G. Gemeunden (2001) "Teamwork quality and the success of innovation projects: A theoretical concept and empirical evidence", *Organization Science*, 12(4, Jul–Aug): 435–49.

54 B. Mullen and C. Copper (1994) "The relation between group cohesiveness and performance: An integration", *Psychological Bulletin*, 115(2): 210–27.

55 M.H. Kernis, B.D. Grannemann, T. Richie and J. Hart (1988) "The role of contextual factors in relationship between physical activity and self-awareness", *British Journal of Social Psychology*, 23: 119–45.

56 P. Cushman (1986) "The self-besieged: Recruitment-indoctrination processes in restrictive groups", Special issue: The rediscovery of self in social psychology, *Journal for the Theory of Social Behavior*, 16: 1–32.

57 F. Wright, X.H. Hoffman and E.M. Gore (1988) "Perspectives on scapegoating in primary groups", *Group*, 12: 33–44.

58 J.M. Oehler and P.Z. Perault (1986) "The process of scapegoating in a neonatal nurses' group", *Group*, 10: 74–84.

59 H.W. Tuckman (1965) "Developmental sequences in small groups", *Psychological Bulletin*, 63: 384–99.

60 C. Gersick (1988) "Time and transition in work teams: Toward a new model of group development", *Academy of Management Journal*, 31: 9–41; (1989) "Marking time: Predictable transitions in task groups", *Academy of Management Journal*, 32(2): 274–309.

Chapter 3

1   J. Whitmore (1996) *Coaching for Performance* (2nd edn) Nicholas Brealey Publishing, London.

2   G. Szulanski (1996) "Exploring internal stickiness: Impediments to the transfer of best practices within the firm", *Strategic Management Journal*, 17(Winter): 27–44.

3   J.R. Hackman and R. Wageman (2005) "A theory of team coaching", *Academy of Management Review*, 30(2): 269–87.

4   R. Wageman, J.R. Hackman and E.V. Lehman (2004) "Development of the Team Diagnostic Survey", working paper, Tuck School, Dartmouth College, Hanover, NH.

5   J.L. Komaki (1986) "Toward effective supervision: An operant analysis and comparison of managers at work", *Journal of Applied Psychology*, 74: 522–9; R.E. Smith, F.L. Smoll and B. Curtis (1979) "Coach effectiveness training: A cognitive-behavioural approach to enhancing relationship skills in youth sport coaches", *Journal of Sport Psychology*, 1: 59–75.

6   R. Schwarz (1994) *Team Facilitation*, Prentice Hall, Englewood Cliffs, NJ.

7   E.H. Schein (1988) *Process Consultation Vol. 1*, Addison-Wesley, Reading, MA.

8   S.W.J. Kozlowski, S.M. Gully, E. Salas and J.A. Cannon-Bowers (1996) "Team leadership and development: Theory, principles and guidelines for training leaders and team", in M. Beyerlein, D. Johnson and S. Beyerlein (eds) *Advances in Interdisciplinary Studies of Work Teams: Team Leadership*, 3: 251–89, JAI Press, Greenwich, CT.

9   H.C. Ginnett (1993) "Crews as groups; Their formation and their leadership", in E.L. Wiener, B.G. Kanki and R.L. Helmreich (eds) *Cockpit Resource Management*, Academic Press, Orlando, FL, pp 71–98.

10 J.R. Hackman, K.R. Brousseau and J.A. Weiss (1976) "The interaction of task design and group performance strategies in determining group effectiveness", *Organizational Behavior and*

Human Performance, 16: 350–65.

11 G. Burns (1995) "The secrets of team facilitation", *Training and Development Journal*, June: 46–52.

12 J.R. Hackmann (1990) "Creating more effective work groups in organizations", in J.R. Hackman (ed.) *Groups that Work (and Those that Don't): Creating Effective Conditions for Teamwork*, Jossey-Bass, San Francisco.

13 D. Lindsley, D. Brass and J. Thomas (1995) "Efficiency-performance spirals: A multi-level perspective", *Academy of Management Review*, 20: 645–78.

14 R. Katz (1982) "The effects of group longevity on project communication and performance", *Administrative Science Quarterly*, 27: 81–104.

15 J. Katzenbach and D. Smith (1993) *The Wisdom of Teams: Creating the High-Performance Organization*, Harper, New York; J. Katzenbach (1998) *Teams at the Top*, Harvard Business School Press, Boston.

16 Senior consultant and certified professional co-active coach Lilliann Andreassen has been working with corporate boards for almost ten years, both as a board member and as a lecturer/project manager. See www.thecoaches.com.

17 P. Zeus and S. Skiffington (2000) *The Complete Guide to Coaching at Work*, McGraw-Hill, Sydney.

18 D. Meier (2005) *Team Coaching with the Solution Circle*, Solutions Books, Cheltenham; M. McKergow and J. Clarke (2005) *Positive Approaches to Change*, Solutions Books, Cheltenham; P.Z. Jackson and M. McKergow (2006) *The Solutions Focus: Making Coaching and Change SIMPLE*, Nicholas Brealey International, London.

Chapter 4

1 C. Argyris (1993) "Education for leader-learning", *Organizational Dynamics*, 21(3): 5–17.

2   A.C. Edmondson (2002) "The local and variegated nature of learning in organizations", *Organization Science*, 13(2, March–April): 128–46.

3   C. Argyris and D. Schon (1996) *Organizational Learning II: Theory, Method, and Practice*, Addison-Wesley Longman, Reading, MA; (1991) "Teaching smart people how to learn", *Harvard Business Review*, 69(3): 99–109.

4   P. Senge (1990) *The Fifth Discipline*, Doubleday, New York.

5   J.S. Bunderson and K.M. Sutcliffe (2003) "Management team learning orientation and business unit orientation", *Journal of Applied Psychology*, 83(3): 552–60.

6   M. van Offenbeek (2001) "Processes and outcomes of team learning", *European Journal of Work and Organizational Psychology*, 10(3): 303–17; G.P. Huber (1991) "Organizational learning: The contributing processes and literatures", *Organization Science*, 1: 88–115.

7   Huber, *op. cit.*

8   C. D'Andrea-O'Brien and A.F. Buono (1996) "Building effective learning teams: Lessons from the field", *SAM Advanced Management Journal*, Summer: 4–9.

9   J.A. Cannon-Bowers, E. Salas and S. Converse (1993) "Shared mental models in expert team decision making", in J. Castellan (ed.) *Current Issues in Individual and Group Decision Making*, Lawrence Erlbaum Associates, Hillsdale, NJ.

10   A. Edmondson (1999) "Psychological safety and learning behavior in work teams", *Administrative Science Quarterly*, 44: 350–83.

11   C. Argyris (1982) *Reasoning, Learning and Action: Individual and Organizational*, Jossey-Bass, San Francisco; F. Lee (1997) "When the going gets tough, do the tough ask for help? Help seeking and power motivations in organizations", *Organizational Behavior and Human Decision Processes*, 72: 336–63; J.P. MacDuffie (1997) "The road to root-cause: Shop-floor problem solving at three auto assembly plants", *Management Science*, 43: 479–502.

12 E.G. Foldy (2004) "Learning from diversity: A theoretical exploration", *Public Administration Review*, 64(5, Sept–Oct): 529–38.

13 R.J. Ely and D.A. Thomas (2001) "Cultural diversity at work: The effects of diversity perspectives on work group processes and outcomes", *Administrative Science Quarterly*, 46(2): 229–73.

14 C. Argyris and D.A. Schon (1974) *Theory in Practice: Increasing Professional Effectiveness*, Jossey-Bass, San Francisco; (1996) *Organizational Learning II: Theory, Method and Practice*, Addison-Wesley, Reading, MA.

15 P.C. Early and E. Mosakowski (2000) "Creating hybrid team cultures: An empirical test of transnational team functioning", *Academy of Management Journal*, 43(1): 26–49.

16 G.S. van Vegt and J.S. Bunderson (2005) "Learning and performance in multidisciplinary teams: The importance of collective team identification", *Academy of Management Journal*, 48(3): 532–47.

17 M. van Offenbeek (2001) "Processes and outcomes of team learning", *European Journal of Work and Organizational Psychology*, 10(3): 303–17.

18 J.W. Rudolph, S.S. Taylor and E.G. Foldy (2001) "Collaborative off-line reflection: A way to develop skill in action science and action inquiry", in P. Reason and H. Bradbury (eds) *Handbook of Action Research*, Sage, London.

19 H.K. Choi and L. Thompson (2005) "Old wine in a new bottle: Impact of membership change on group creativity", *Organizational Behavior and Human Decision Processes*, 98: 121–32.

20 D. Goleman (1996) *Vital Lies, Simple Truths: The Psychology of Self-Deception*, Touchstone Books, Sutton Valence.

21 C. Gersick (1998) "Time and transition in work teams: Toward a new model of group development", *Academy of Management Journal*, 31(1): 9–41.

22 G.P. Huber (1999) "Facilitating project team learning and

contributions to organizational knowledge", *Creativity and Innovation Management*, 8(2, June): 70–6.

23 P.J. Lane and M. Lubatkin (1998) "Relative absorptive capacity and interorganizational learning", *Strategic Management Journal*, 19: 461–77.

24 D.L. Duarte and N.T. Snyder (2001) *Mastering Virtual Teams*, Jossey-Bass, San Francisco.

25 T.K. Lant (1992) "Aspiration-level adaptation: An empirical exploration", *Management Science*, 38(5): 623–44.

26 A.C. Edmondson (2002) "The local and variegated nature of learning in organizations", *Organization Science*, 13(2, March–April): 128–46.

27 C.J. Gersick and J.R. Hackman (1990) "Habitual routines in task-performing teams", *Organization Behavior and Human Decision Processes*, 47(1): 65–97.

28 D. Kim (1993) "The link between individual and organizational learning", *Sloan Management Review*, 35(1, Fall): 37–50.

29 C. D'Andrea-O'Brien and A.F. Buono (1996) "Building effective learning teams: Lessons from the field", *SAM Advanced Management Journal*, Summer: 4–9.

Chapter 5

1 M. Downey (2003) *Effective Coaching* (2nd edn), Texere, London.

2 H. Gardner (1975) *The Shattered Mind*, Knopf, New York; T. Hatch and H. Gardner (1993) "Finding cognition in the classroom: An expanded view of human intelligence", in G. Salomon (ed.) *Distributed Cognitions: Psychological and Educational Considerations*, Cambridge: Cambridge University Press.

3 Downey, *op. cit*.

4 H. Benson (2005) "Are you working too hard?", *Harvard Business Review*, November: 53–8.

5 D.A. Kolb (1984) *Experimental Learning: Experience as the*

Source of Learning and Development, Prentice-Hall, New Jersey.

6   S. Berglas (2004) "Chronic time abuse", *Harvard Business Review*, June: 90–7.

7   D.G. Ancona and D.F. Caldwell (1992) "Bridging the boundary: External activity and performance in organizational teams", *Administrative Science Quarterly*, 37: 634–65.

8   Action Profile Decision Framing is based on the work of Rudolph Laban, Warren Lamb and Pamela Ramsden, among others.

Chapter 6

1   D. Clutterbuck and D. Megginson (2005) *Coaching at Work*, CIPD, Wimbledon.

2   M. Belbin (2003) *Management Teams: Why They Succeed or Fail* (2nd edn), Butterworth Heinemann, Oxford.

3   C. Margerison and D. McCann (2000) *Team Management: Practical New Approaches*, Management Books, London; Margerison-McCann Team Management Index, available from www.changingminds.org.

Index